FILM STARS

Stars are an integral part of every major film industry in the world. In this pivotal new series, each book is devoted to an international movie star, looking at the development of their identity, their acting and performance methods, the cultural significance of their work, and their influence and legacy. Taking a wide range of different stars, including George Clooney, Brigitte Bardot and Dirk Bogarde amongst others, this series encompasses the sphere of silent and sound acting, Hollywood and non-Hollywood areas of cinema, and child and adult forms of stardom. With its broad range, but a focus throughout on the national and historical dimensions to film, the series offers students and researchers a new approach to studying film.

SERIES EDITORS
Martin Shingler and Susan Smith

PUBLISHED TITLES

Barbara Stanwyck *Andrew Klevan*
Brigitte Bardot *Ginette Vincendeau*
Carmen Miranda *Lisa Shaw*
Elizabeth Taylor *Susan Smith*
Nicole Kidman *Pam Cook*
Star Studies: A Critical Guide *Martin Shingler*

Forthcoming
Penélope Cruz *Ann Davies*

Mickey ROURKE

KERI WALSH

palgrave
màcmillan

A BFI book published by Palgrave Macmillan

First published in 2014 by
PALGRAVE MACMILLAN

on behalf of the

BRITISH FILM INSTITUTE
21 Stephen Street, London W1T 1LN
www.bfi.org.uk

There's more to discover about film and television through the BFI. Our world-renowned archive, cinemas, festivals, films, publications and learning resources are here to inspire you.

Palgrave Macmillan in the UK is an imprint of Macmillan Publishers Limited, registered in England, company number 785998, of Houndmills, Basingstoke, Hampshire RG21 6XS. Palgrave Macmillan in the US is a division of St Martin's Press LLC, 175 Fifth Avenue, New York, NY 10010. Palgrave Macmillan is the global academic imprint of the above companies and has companies and representatives throughout the world. Palgrave® and Macmillan® are registered trademarks in the United States, the United Kingdom, Europe and other countries.

Designed by couch
Cover images: (front) *9½ Weeks* (Adrian Lyne, 1986), Jonesfilm/Galactic Films/Triple Ajaxxx; (back) *The Wrestler* (Darren Aronofsky, 2008), © Off the Top Rope, Inc./© Wild Bunch

Set by Cambrian Typesetters, Camberley, Surrey
Printed in China

This book is printed on paper suitable for recycling and made from fully managed and sustained forest sources. Logging, pulping and manufacturing processes are expected to conform to the environmental regulations of the country of origin.

British Library Cataloguing-in-Publication Data
A catalogue record for this book is available from the British Library
A catalog record for this book is available from the Library of Congress

ISBN 978–1–84457–430–8 (pb)

CONTENTS

ACKNOWLEDGMENTS

Thanks to Audrey Bilger, James Morrison, John Farrell, Shonni Enelow, Sarah Zimmerman, Moshe Gold, Evan Kindley, Briallen Hopper, Kevin Lamb, Ron Levao, Susan Wolfson, Daniel Larlham, Richard Brody, Cheryl Pawelski, Peter Manning, Michael Eklund, Megan Bennett, David Yaffe and John Bugg.

Martin Shingler has been a singularly patient and convivial editor, and I hope we get a chance to work together again soon. I'm also grateful to Susan Smith, Sophia Contento, Rebecca Barden, Philippa Hudson and Lucinda Knight for their excellent work on the BFI Film Stars series.

INTRODUCTION

Why watch Mickey Rourke? There are many ways of approaching this question, and in the course of writing about him one encounters some recurring – and frequently passionate – answers: because he is an intense and magnetic performer; because he has an elusive quality on screen that keeps one following his career despite its low patches; because, as Deborah Ross put it in *The Independent* in 2003, 'he used to be so gorgeous, like a James Dean gone to seed in the most shaggable way';[1] because he's an 'actor's actor' who brings rare creativity and depth to the craft; because he's a risk-taker and refreshing critic of the industry. In life, Rourke often seems hounded by personal demons, but every now and then he is able to discipline his wild energy into moments of acute insight, empathy and self-revelation that make for thrilling performances. Over the course of his thirty-five-year career, Rourke has been many things to many people: the brightest young star out of the Actors Studio, a Hollywood hotshot, a Hollywood has-been, a professional boxer, a plastic surgery victim, an independent film-maker's muse, a Comic-Con icon and, most recently, an eccentric thespian and grand old man.

There were those for whom Rourke's comeback in Darren Aronofsky's *The Wrestler* (2008) was no surprise: they remembered his charismatic screen presence, his bad behaviour of the late 1980s had transformed from recent scandal to Hollywood legend, and they welcomed him back at the top of his game. There were others who remembered him less favourably, and who cringed at his flesh-exposing, masochistic performance as a washed-up athlete. And then there were others, like me, who had been just a bit too young in the 1980s really to know who Rourke was, but for whom the decade still exerted the powerful pull of the culture of one's youth. Getting drawn into Rourke's filmography after being captivated by his performance in *The Wrestler*, I watched him age in reverse, marvelling in the revealed treasures of his work in *Body Heat, Diner, 9½ Weeks, Barfly, Johnny Handsome* and a range of other films I'd missed the first time around. What I found was that Mickey Rourke's performances – his thoughtful characterisations, his detailed and loving portraits of blue-collar life, and his push against the dominant values of his era – brought greater texture and quality to the popular culture he inhabited. His characters were scruffy, self-destructive and downwardly mobile, but in his early roles his performances were grounded in a sweetness that made his characters likeable in spite of their faults. Looking back at his career from the perspective of the twenty-first century, it is clear that though his body of work has been idiosyncratic and uneven, and though it sometimes seems that he has missed more opportunities than he has taken advantage of, Rourke has nonetheless enriched American cinema since the 1980s with a magnetic inscrutability that very few actors possess.

By any reasonable standard, Rourke has bad career judgment. He is said to have turned down what became two star-making parts for Tom Cruise (in *Top Gun* [1986] and *Born on the Fourth of July* [1989]). He also, for one reason or another, sat out *Dead Poets Society* (1989), *Platoon* (1986), *Rain Man* (1988), *The Untouchables* (1987), and later, roles in Quentin Tarantino's *Pulp Fiction* (1994) and *Grindhouse* (2007). Any one of these films would have been a superb showcase for his talent. But who can understand the mysterious ways of Mickey Rourke? If he had done what his teachers, agents and fans expected of him and taken these roles, he wouldn't be Mickey

Rourke. He's an idiosyncratic actor who makes unexpected choices, some out of principle and artistic preference, and others simply because he can't seem to drag himself out of bed in the morning. But even if the young Rourke made some questionable decisions, he zealously guarded his artistic credibility – until, suddenly, he didn't. And even in films as imperfect as *Rumble Fish* (1983) and *Angel Heart* (1987), Rourke reminded moviegoers of the old-fashioned thrills that could come from watching a serious actor framed as a matinee idol.

In an age of prep, Rourke was never preppy. He not only cared about acting, he cared about being cool, especially in the early days, taking roles in films that allowed him to out-hip his screen mates. He made leading man William Hurt look like a wet noodle in *Body Heat* (1981), performed street cred against the suburban sweetness of the cast of *Diner* (1982) and played the charismatic centre of a gang in *Rumble Fish*. He pulled out all the hipster stops to play the California beat icon Charles Bukowski's fictional alter ego in *Barfly* (1987). In that film he showed how well he knew the arts of the gutter. His acting pulsed with sexual melancholy: he was always losing the girl, and maybe wasn't even sure he wanted her. Like all of the most intriguing sex symbols, there was something unlikely about him – he wasn't a conventional leading man, he wasn't a smooth talker and he certainly wasn't an effective rescuer of women. But he had what Pauline Kael called 'a sweet, pure smile that surprises you', and he played a variation on what he was: a kid from the wrong side of the tracks, lacking opportunities, in danger of screwing up his life and always looking for a protector.[2] He was a would-be mama's boy who lacked a mama, and whose characters tried to hide their wounds behind a series of tough exteriors: gambling, boxing, womanising, motorcycles, tattoos. In life, Rourke seemed to be a self-destructive risk-taker, but on film, the artistic risks he took were rewarded, and whenever he opened his heart to an audience, it responded with love and affection.

Mickey Rourke is an enigmatic star who has spent a lifetime trying to hide from exposure, all the while seeming compulsively driven to expose himself. Call him an exhibitionist introvert. Today Rourke has the aura of a grizzled survivor, an ancient mariner who has suffered all the blows that life, boxing and the film industry have to offer. But the young Rourke was anything but a tough guy. Before arriving in New York, he was a shy graduate of Miami Beach Senior High from an abusive home.[3] Rourke grew up in the shadow of Muhammad Ali, who had boxed at his neighbourhood's 5th Street Gym, but concussions diverted him from pursuing his dream of professional boxing. According to those who knew him at the time, he was something like the characters he would play in his early films: funny and sweet, anxious and lonely, introverted and curious, smarter than he looked, but not as tough or worldly-wise as he would have people believe. His origins as a performer were accidental. When a cast member dropped out of his friend's student production of Jean Genet's *Deathwatch*, Rourke had been roped into the role of Green Eyes. It was a fortuitous part, as he found in Genet's world – the moral inversions, vindications of criminality, complex layerings of identity, queerness and kink – both a terrain he recognised from his own experiences on the streets of Miami, and a gateway to new and more fluid ways of identifying and desiring through performance. The experience of playing the sexually charismatic Green Eyes was so transformative that he was willing to stake his future on it: he left Miami for the New York theatre world.

Coming north in the early 1970s was in some sense a return home: Rouke had been born in Schenectady, and had moved to Miami with his mother, brother and sister when he was six years old, after his parents' divorce. Born Philip Andre Rourke on 16 September 1952, he was named after his father, Philip Rourke, a carpenter and an enthusiastic bodybuilder who, according to one account, gave him the nickname 'Mickey' in honour of Mickey

Mantle (by Rourke's own account in 2010, he got the nickname because 'my mother hated my father, and we had the same name'). When his mother remarried, it was to a Miami Beach cop who already had five sons of his own. Their household was violent, and Rourke and his younger brother Joe were his stepfather's frequent targets.[4] Rourke learned street smarts by necessity and became passionate about sports, through which he thought he could toughen up and deal with the damage inflicted by his upbringing, and maybe even escape from his own skin.

Rourke poured his anxieties, anger and yearning into his work on stage, where the very vacancies and caverns in his identity would contribute to his empathy and fluidity as a performer. It would be a decade-long journey to his first film roles. Nor did his admission to the Actors Studio come easily (not a training institution, the Actors Studio is a work space for actors, so first Rourke had to learn how to act). His first acting teacher was Walter Lott, with whom he worked before becoming a student of Sandra Seacat, who would become his most inspiring coach and mentor. He took the kind of odd jobs that starving actors take, working as a towel boy in a massage parlour, selling nuts from a cart on the street, unloading boxes down at the docks and training attack dogs. He swiped chocolate bars from grocery stores and lived on whatever he could scrounge up, his life often intersecting closely with those of the hustlers and johns of the Marlton Hotel where he lived for a spell. After studying for several years with Seacat, Rourke was admitted to the Actors Studio following his first audition – an unusual feat, when one considers that Jack Nicholson auditioned five times.

From this auspicious beginning, he would hit the height of his star power in Adrian Lyne's *9½ Weeks* (1986), which, with its domesticated kink and Wall Street chic, became an iconic piece of 1980s pop culture. He's been a multi-millionaire and he's been a bum. His star image is that he's never been able to conform to a star image. He's a perpetual lost boy, by turns self-deprecating and self-aggrandising, a shy and often self-destructive actor who has thrown away more than he's kept, spent more than he's earned and who, when not turning in one of his rare, mesmerising performances, gives the impression of someone simply not able to live up to his potential. But even when he stuns critics as he did in *Barfly* and *The Wrestler*, he tends to be undervalued by the industry. Perhaps it's because he cultivates misunderstoodness by grumbling about Hollywood 'politics' and 'bullshit'. Or perhaps it's because of the kind of films he makes, which are almost always difficult to place in the high/low culture divide. His films are unpredictable at the box office, and he has never won an Academy Award. One of Darren Aronofsky's frequent laments on the interview circuit for *The Wrestler* was just how hard it was to raise money on Mickey Rourke's name.

When Pauline Kael saw Rourke in Barry Levinson's *Diner*, she described his performance as having an 'off-kilter' quality. His casting in that film was certainly 'off-kilter' – he played a Jewish college kid while looking like an Irish thirty-year-old, a 1950s gambling addict who wore glam-rock-inspired eyeliner. Such casting, wardrobe and period dysphorias have remained a hallmark of Rourke's career, as he has never shied away from playing a role simply because it didn't correspond to his age or physical type. But his path has been 'off-kilter' in others ways as well. Despite being the actor whom Elia Kazan supposedly lauded for delivering the best audition the Actors Studio had seen in thirty years, and despite gaining wide acclaim as one of the finest actors working in film, Rourke has always seemed generationally out of sync in Hollywood, arriving too late to play the streetwise 1970s Pacino/Keitel-style roles he had been groomed for, and too early for the counter-cultural independent films of the 1990s. Though Rourke has worked in many genres without claiming one as his own, he has nonetheless forged a distinctive star image that combines 1950s rebel, rock star, blue-collar anti-hero and bohemian.

On screen, Rourke can be a magician, making a role matter and a character come to life in a way few actors can. But his niche is hard to pin down. He's not a moral compass like Sean Penn, nor a classic movie star like Paul Newman or George Clooney. He can't disappear into a role like Ben Kingsley or Meryl Streep. At times he gives the impression of being too consumed with life to be a professional actor – too busy bonding with boxers and taking care of his dogs, and too busy fighting his depression, anxiety and low self-esteem. But when he gets in front of the camera with the right director, in the right frame of mind, he hits it like no one else can. Like the compelling deadbeats he's played, his star image is that he's a day late and a dollar short, but he's always worth waiting for.

Rourke has less catlike resilience than Robert Downey Jr and more soul than Tom Cruise. He has as deep a commitment to 'living the role' through intensive research as Daniel Day-Lewis. Perhaps his closest cousin is Johnny Depp, a Rourke admirer who took up the mantle of Rourke's kinkiness and turned toward the eccentric world of Tim Burton, forging a stranger but more cohesive cult image. Other kindred spirits might have been River Phoenix or Heath Ledger (fellow lost boys), or Russell Crowe or Colin Farrell (similarly drawn to the boxing ring). Certainly, his name belongs in the list that includes Marlon Brando, James Dean and Montgomery Clift, as well as the tradition of character actors like Charles Laughton and tough guys like Humphrey Bogart and Clint Eastwood. But to best comprehend his career, it is helpful to think of Mickey Rourke as an actor of the 1970s who made it big in the 1980s. If you watch his films closely, you'll see how often he hams it up in playful tribute to 1970s masters like Robert De Niro, Al Pacino and Harvey Keitel, with hand gestures, elaborate borough accents and scenes played over plates of spaghetti. As Rourke told an interviewer in 2008, referring to his slightly older colleagues at the Actors Studio: 'Looking around in that little tiny building and seeing these guys? I shook in my fucking dirty blue jeans. I mean, those were the gods. They were the role models, and they still are.'[5] Like many kids of his generation, he was inspired by the vision of New York City he found in the films of Scorsese and Coppola, an inverse glamour of seediness, hunger, violence and despair. It was an era that valued eccentricity in its actors, that privileged intensity and interestingness over good looks, and that allowed for a wider range of accents and ethnicities than Hollywood film had ever allowed before. The iconic male performances of the era – Dustin Hoffman and Jon Voight in *Midnight Cowboy* (1969), Al Pacino and Marlon Brando in *The Godfather* (1972), Robert De Niro and Harvey Keitel in *Mean Streets* (1973) – generated a vision of New York as a hostile landscape where survival took every ounce of one's strength. In this violent world, bonds between men and women were hopeless, while bonds between men, though sometimes beautiful and tenacious, were threatened on every side. Post-Vietnam urban male isolation and rage were captured definitively by De Niro's 1976 performance as Travis Bickle, the homicidal anti-hero of *Taxi Driver*. It was the era of Italian-American cinema (Coppola, Scorsese and Cimino), but also of Robert Altman, Woody Allen, Terrence Malick and John Sayles. And there were intimations of a new kind of film-making in the work of talented upstarts like George Lucas and Steven Spielberg. Their West Coast aesthetic of adventuresome blockbusters like *Jaws* (1975) and *Star Wars* (1977) took its place alongside the gritty urban realism that had defined the 1970s and would continue to thrive in films like *Scarface* (1983) and the *Rocky* series. With its rock 'n' roll soundtrack, innovative filming techniques and strong ensemble cast, *Mean Streets* was perhaps the decade's definitive coming-of-age film.

This was the period, and this was the New York City – both imaginary and real – that Mickey Rourke came seeking when he borrowed money from his sister for a plane ticket from Miami. He found the streets abuzz with the same mythic, criminal energies he had seen on the screen. As he told David Letterman in 2008, he arrived in New York 'when Times Square was still Times Square':

a land of porn theatres, petty crime and hustlers, before 42nd Street had become hospitable to tourists. As the grit of the 1970s film renaissance morphed into the more conventionally glamorous commercialism of the 1980s, we can see the roots – and some of the tensions – of Rourke's career. He came out of the Actors Studio with the fierce, independent, vernacular values of the 1970s. He was a few years older than the Brat Pack with whom he competed for roles, and he had to make his way in the glossy films of the 1980s. He worked with legendary 1970s directors whenever he could, beginning with a small part in Cimino's over-budget flop *Heaven's Gate* (1980), then with Coppola on *Rumble Fish*, and again with Cimino on *Year of the Dragon* (1985). But he had missed the 1970s boat, and instead ended up making his biggest impact as a star with a distinctively 1980s flavour in films where he appeared tough mostly because he was surrounded by nice suburban kids. Adrian Lyne's *9½ Weeks* presented a decidedly 1980s version of Manhattan: gone were the tawdry but lovable streets of 1970s New York cinema – now the criminals were inside the Wall Street skyscrapers. Lyne presented New York in the same light as *Wall Street* (1987) and *Bright Lights Big City* (1988), as a land of limitless wealth but spiritual deadness, where anonymous intimacies among stockbrokers and bored divorcees unfolded against a backdrop of designer clothes, commodities, fog and romantic, filtered lenses, set to a soundtrack of synthesised pop. Rourke's character John (no surname) inhabits this corporate landscape as an enigma whose personality and desires are never fully revealed. John's identity is a mystery that Kim Basinger's character Elizabeth tries to solve by peering into his closets and drawers, but even these intimate spaces don't reveal the secrets of the man whose spell she has fallen under. Like his character in that film, Rourke is a mysterious performer. Some elements of his screen charisma may perpetually elude categorisation. But if we study his career and its cultural and cinematic contexts closely, we can come to a greater understanding of the reasons why Rourke, both as an actor and as a star, has intrigued audiences for so long.

1 METHOD ACTOR

If you don't got dreams, Bagel, you got nightmares.

Boogie Sheftell, *Diner*

Rourke emerged as a star by playing variations on a type the film
critic Richard Dyer has called 'the sad young man'. In his essay
'Coming Out as Going In', Dyer uses the career of Montgomery
Clift as the chief example of this figure in cinema. 'The sad young
man' is a young man on the threshold of discovering his
homosexuality. He forms a counterpoint to the 'angry young man' of
the 1950s typified by such figures as Richard Burton's Jimmy Porter
in *Look Back in Anger* (1958) or Marlon Brando's Johnny Strabler in
The Wild One (1953). In Dyer's formulation, 'the sad young man
image is frozen on the moment before "becoming" or knowing that
one "is" a queer'. Dyer suggests that the image – found also in pulp
and literary fiction, and dating at least as far back as the Romantic
poets – is 'an important element in highly public star images such as
Montgomery Clift, Sal Mineo, James Dean', and he notes 'the strong
sense of the sad young man's desirability to heterosexual women'.
This desirability comes partly from the sad young man's femininity,
but also from his withdrawal, his complexity and his sensitivity.
'The sad young man is a figure of romance/pornography', notes
Dyer, a point that is crucial for comprehending Rourke's career at
the beginning of the 1980s and beyond.[1]

The early Rourke always hovered on this threshold, lyrical, mysteriously distracted, ultimately unavailable. He was defined by his fluidity, and he could engage sexual attention from all directions, holding out a rich sense of sexual possibility. In a memorably charged scene in *Diner*, for instance, his character throws his head back to drink a stream of sugar provocatively from a dispenser, thereby bringing a conversation about his friend's virginity to a homoerotic halt. But he was also a figure of foreclosure, and of a sense that time was running out, and that moving definitively to 'adulthood' would involve losses and compromises that might be too hard to bear. Rourke's films of the early 1980s suggest a range of unhappy futures – none of them beyond the closet – for the sad young man. In *Body Heat*, his future is jail. In *Diner*, the possibility of a normative heterosexual future is floated, but Rourke's love object is far enough out of his league to make it seem unlikely. In *Rumble Fish*, his character dies at the hands of police, while in *The Pope of Greenwich Village* (1984) it becomes apparent that sentimental bonds between men might be able to compensate for, and maybe even coexist with, the pressures of heterosexuality, fatherhood and failed relationships with women.

In all of his early roles, Rourke played characters suspended for longer than felt comfortable in the period between adolescence and adulthood. He played characters who weren't interested in living up to the cultural scripts that awaited them. *Diner* highlighted Rourke's femininity as the key source of his success with women, but also, and increasingly, as a source of shame that must be covered up. Vincent Canby noticed this dynamic when he called Rourke in *Diner* 'the most interesting of the lot' and explains that 'Boogie (Mickey Rourke), who works as a hairdresser by day, is deeply in debt to the bookies, and pretends to be studying law by night, in this way to neutralise some of the more unpleasant associations that attach to the reputation of male hairdressers'.[2] Levinson leaves Boogie's future unknown, but at the film's end (in an attempt to contain his femininity and recklessness with money), he is rescued by a town elder and father figure (a friend of his mother's) from his gambling debts, and offered a more suitably masculine job in construction. Boogie accepts this temporarily, but warns his mother's friend that he can't be relied on to stick around for long, because (as he explains cryptically) 'You know, I got plans.'

'I see you had a misspent youth', Elizabeth Taylor tells pool shark Montgomery Clift in George Stevens's *A Place in the Sun* (1951). Watching the film in his high-school English class, Rourke was captivated by Clift's presence and would study his acting closely, introducing similar qualities into his performances in *Diner* and *Rumble Fish*.[3] Rourke was often compared to Brando in the early days of his career, but a comparison with Clift seems most appropriate, since Rourke was introspective and introverted like Clift, rather than earthy and uninhibited like Brando. Steve Vineberg identifies the qualities Clift brings to his role in *A Place in the Sun* as 'forceful erotic charge' combined with 'laconic expressiveness', and a 'gift for communicating the feelings of a hypersensitive and inarticulate character'.[4] These are the qualities that inspired Rourke's version of Method.

Clift's performances of the late 1940s and early 1950s were defining moments in Method acting style. 'Method acting' is a complex notion that means many things, and about which many actors, directors and audiences have strong feelings. It is a form of realist acting, and today many teachers use the broader term 'Stanislavski-based system' to refer to the kinds of approaches that are popularly deemed 'Method'. In popular culture, the term 'Method' evokes an American acting tradition that goes from John Garfield through Dean, Clift and Brando to De Niro, Pacino, Hoffman and beyond. In this sense, 'Method' refers both to a loose set of rubrics governing preparation for a role, and also to the creative communities surrounding certain influential teachers such as Lee Strasberg (of the Actors Studio) and Stella

Adler (of The Stella Adler Studio of Acting). Keeping in mind that 'Method acting' encompasses different approaches, and also that it is only one strain of Stanislavski-based acting, I will try to delineate some of the ways in which Rourke's career is recognisably 'Method'.

Method acting has frequently been the source of satire for the lengths its actors go to 'live' a role, from tales of De Niro's twelve-hour taxi-driving shifts in preparation for his role as Travis Bickle, to Hoffman's epic runs before filming scenes for *Marathon Man* (1976). It was Hoffman's jogs that sparked Laurence Olivier's apocryphal remark, 'Why not try acting? It's a lot easier.' Well, why not try 'acting' in this conventional sense? Because practitioners of the Method strive for verisimilitude, seeking to narrow the gap between art and life as much as possible. In a study of the acting style and its practitioners, Steve Vineberg has compiled a useful list of its governing features.[5] Privileging displays of genuine emotion, Method acting uses the personal experiences of the actor as the material from which performances are drawn. In keeping with the ideas developed by Konstantin Stanislavski at the Moscow Art Theatre at the turn of the twentieth century, it makes use of improvisation and spontaneity. Typically, Method acting preparation aims at inner transformations and insights, and is not vocational or directed toward any particular kind of performance (in fact, the process-oriented nature of the work at the Actors Studio confused Rourke – he wondered why so few of his fellow members worked professionally as actors). Method performers strive for intimate communication between themselves and other actors in a scene. They make frequent use of physical objects as props, as a form of both naturalism and symbolism. They also have a tendency to describe the craft as more than a job, as a quasi-religious or mystical devotion to the process of finding truth in the theatre. This last factor, in combination with Method's attraction to objects, perhaps helps to explain the fetishism that has accumulated around the acting style.

In Method acting, the use of the personal life and experiences of the actor is key, as opposed to 'technique' learned or transmitted from one performer to another (as in traditions like ballet, for instance, where the individuality of performers is less important than their discipline to the form). As Stanislavski put it, 'The form and setting will vary according to the play, but the actor's human emotions, which run parallel to the feelings of the role, must remain alive. They must not be faked or replaced by something else, some convoluted actors' trick.'[6] In a Method performance, you don't try to become someone else, but to find ways of connecting your own experiences to those of your character. Developing a character, Method actors typically begin inside themselves and work outward, an inversion of the classical British style (Laurence Olivier always worked by preparing the physical appearance of a character first – he knew he had found his character when he found the right nose). As a student of Sandra Seacat and then as a member of the Actors Studio, Rourke learned Method principles such as improvisation, acting 'as if', and 'living the role' by conducting deep research into characters (and he still draws on these techniques: for his performance as Whiplash in *Iron Man 2* [2010], for instance, Rourke visited a Russian prison). Method acting is the foundation of all Rourke performances, both as a technique and as a recurring set of themes and preoccupations: the family, social class, abuse and abandonment, heterosexuality and its discontents, and the emotional upheavals of failed masculinity.

The most significant controversy in Method acting pedagogy is based around the rift between its two most influential teachers, Stella Adler and Lee Strasberg, and the relative importance that should be placed on 'affective memory' (sometimes called 'emotion memory') in acting. Affective memory is a style of calling up the past through the contemplation of objects or experiences, and deploying those recovered emotions for the purposes of developing a character and generating emotional truths in performance. Based on

Rourke's comments about his manner of working (for instance, he has mentioned having his first acting breakthrough while contemplating a pair of boxing shoes), it seems that he follows a non-dogmatic version of the Strasberg school. His studies with Sandra Seacat appear to have included variations on Strasberg's 'emotion memory' exercises. In an interview about Elia Kazan, Seacat remarked:

I did an affective memory at the Actors Studio years ago, after which Lee Strasberg said, 'Now *that's* an affective memory. Darling, tell them how you did it.' When I explained my process, Strasberg replied, 'That's not how you do an affective memory! But that's what the Method is all about. It's a way of work!' You find your own way of carrying out your own and your character's internal truth – within your body, mind, and soul.[7]

The foundational personal experiences through which Rourke found himself as an actor involved his relationship with his father. 'It is your own individual experiences, which you bring to the role from the real world that give it life', wrote Stanislavksi, and to develop as a Method actor, Rourke had to muster the courage to revisit his own past.[8] Near the beginning of his career, with Seacat's encouragement, Rourke made the kind of difficult emotional odyssey that characterises Method practice, when he travelled to Schenectady, New York, to seek out his father, Philip Rourke. This emotional courage was necessary to prepare for an important audition. He described his reunion with his father to James Lipton during his appearance on *Inside the Actors Studio*:

LIPTON: How did you find him?
ROURKE: This is the part that's really weird. We used to go eat, when we were little, in this hamburger place, White Castle, so I walked up State Street and I walked into the White Castle ...
LIPTON: State Street where?

ROURKE: Schenectady, upstate. And I sat down, I had a hamburger, and I was just lookin' around at the people that were sitting there, and I seen this one dude, and I was looking at his back and his hands, I don't know, there was something familiar, I said 'fuck, he's right here when I walked in.' And he got up and walked out the door, and I couldn't move, my legs weren't going, and I watched, he stayed at the red light twice, and then I walked out, I remember we were like the same size, and I didn't want to be the same size, so I walked in the gutter. I looked up at him and I said, 'Are you duh-duh-duh,' and he said, 'Yeah.' And then he said to me, he had sunglasses on, and he says, 'I always knew you'd come one day.' We went across the street, we spoke for seven, um, about seven hours, and he gave me fifty bucks and bought me pork chops and mashed potatoes and sauerkraut and he had twenty-two screwdrivers, and that was the last I ever seen him.[9]

As Rourke tells the story, this excursion was aimed directly at gaining the emotional insights he would need for his audition to play Brick in an Actors Studio production of Tennessee Williams's *Cat on a Hot Tin Roof*, the story of a powerful, disapproving father and the son who can't live up to his expectations.

If Rourke's career has been Method in its technique and guiding artistic principles, it has also been Method in a pop-cultural sense: he has enthusiastically embraced the trappings of the Method actor in the popular imagination, from white undershirts to motorcycles to bongo drums, a set of signifiers that announces working-class identity, bohemianism and primitivism. His career has also been highly influenced by the Method's fascination with ethnicity. Rourke has played a variety of roles within the ethnic spectrum of New York's boroughs (Jewish, Irish, Italian, Polish) and has also drawn upon his Florida upbringing to flirt with the culturally charged figure of the white Southerner.

The theme of abandoning fathers supplied the material for most of the memorable parts of Rourke's early career. He has played both sides of the relationship: the abandoned son (*Rumble Fish, Diner, Homeboy, Bullet*), and the abusive and/or abandoning father (*Rape and Marriage, The Pope of Greenwich Village, Angel Heart, The Wrestler*). The pursuit of one's true parentage is a particularly Freudian theme, and Rourke is indeed a Freudian (and Sophoclean) actor. In *Angel Heart*, he acts out the incestuous plot of *Oedipus* in reverse, when he unknowingly has sex with his own daughter. Guilt is one of his major preoccupations, particularly the guilt of the bystander or fellow abused child in an abusive home. The unusual amount of consistency in Rourke's roles indicates that he has taken care to select scripts that matter to him personally and that speak to his interests and strengths as an actor.

Love in the Hamptons (1976)

Rourke's first appearance on screen was in the amateur production *Love in the Hamptons*, Tom Folino's short film based on a 1972 *New Yorker* story of the same name by Elaine Mueller. This half-hour film is about two workers in a hotel bar who begin an affair: an abused wife (Sandy), played by Mary Armstrong, and a younger man (Swede) who wants to save her, played by Rourke. *Love in the Hamptons* gives us our first glimpse of Rourke on film, and here we find none of the swagger he would bring to his later starring roles. The film is highly naturalistic and decidedly a student affair. Rourke first appears on screen when his character Swede arrives by train to work at the Hamptons hotel: he is in profile, eyes cast down, looking like pretty much any 1970s kid, with feathered hair, jeans and a red shirt. He looks up briefly at the camera, and we catch a glimpse of his pasty skin and awkwardly pursed lips. A poor kid from

Tom Folino's *Love in the Hamptons* (1976).
Rourke's first appearance on screen

Brooklyn trying to make it in a rich world, Swede looks in a posh
shop window, then keeps moving. 'Blue cheese? Oil and vinegar?
French?' – these are his first words on screen, as he brings some
stuffy diners their salads. The timbre of his voice is high, and he
seems scared to let loose and act. In the first dramatic action of the
film, his character must make an important decision: when his boss
asks 'What time did she get in today?' (referring to Sandy), Swede
must choose between lying or exposing the lateness of his co-worker.
Nervously playing with the glass he's carrying, he answers vaguely,
'5:30? 6 o'clock? I don't know.' Increasingly concerned for Sandy's
welfare, he asks around at the hotel, curious about whether the
woman's husband might be 'beating on her'. A fellow worker
dismisses his concerns, saying she 'probably likes it', but Swede is
drawn toward the victimised woman. We learn that Swede's
solicitude stems from his own family experiences, as his sister is in an

abusive relationship. In a conversation with his mother, Swede insists: 'She should leave him. He's a goddamn drunken maniac, and I'm sick of having him in the family.'

When he returns to work, his male colleagues are still laughing about Sandy's situation, wondering whether her husband 'put her in the hospital again'. By caring about her, Rourke is established – as he would later be in *Diner* – as the one sensitive male in a world of immature and rowdy guys. As he watches Sandy wait tables with a black eye, he is more and more drawn to her. They become confidantes, stealing alcohol from the bar and setting off to get drunk together. Swede asks, 'Why don't you leave him?', but Sandy doesn't see any viable options. At this point, we get a brief glimmer of Mickey Rourke the star: he looks up at her, shyly and playfully at once, pans her up and down, and then, like a boy trying on something for size, says with a twinkle in his eye, 'I'll take you away if you want to go.' She smiles for the first time in the film, charmed at the offer, and asks, curiously, 'where?' It's a preview of Rourke playing opposite Ellen Barkin in *Diner* as the would-be chivalrous rescuer who is clearly out of his league. 'I always thought that I'd like to go to Alaska,' he responds. When Sandy asks, pragmatically, 'What would you do in Alaska?', he replies, 'What do I do here?'

Near the end of the film, as Swede prepares to run away with Sandy, he shaves and gets dressed, giving Rourke the opportunity to do some Actors Studio-influenced 'private moment' acting. Next, as he waits for her in a bar, he fusses with his drink and the window dressing. We notice Rourke's use of objects (also a legacy of his time at the Actors Studio): in every scene he is grabbing onto something – a glass, a beer can, a cigarette, a knife that he jabs repeatedly into a log on the beach. In the end, Sandy never shows up, and his character receives another sad lesson in the dynamics of abuse.

In *Love in the Hamptons*, Rourke is clearly the best actor on the screen, but his performance is underwhelming, little more than excellent student work. His star quality is evident only in brief snatches, like the promise of something that might thrive if drawn out further. The film does, however, forecast the kind of parts to which Rourke would be attracted, with its themes of domestic violence, marginal characters brought together by loneliness, survivor guilt and the difficulty of ending abusive relationships. The same themes would recur in his performance in the TV movie *Rape and Marriage: The Rideout Case* (1980), where Rourke played John Rideout, the first American man convicted for raping his wife. His co-star was Linda Hamilton, and both turned in frighteningly realistic performances. Whether playing the rescuer of the abused wife or the violent husband, Rourke's early acting roles were concerned with understanding the dynamics of sexual violence in families. Many of his defining roles would find him cast either as sexual predator (*9½ Weeks*, *Angel Heart*) or as witness but ultimately ineffectual rescuer (*Diner*, *Rumble Fish*).

Body Heat (1981)

After his phenomenal successes as screenwriter of *The Empire Strikes Back* (1980) and *Raiders of the Lost Ark* (1981), Lawrence Kasdan took the reins as the director of *Body Heat*. The film's male lead, Juilliard-trained William Hurt, was poised on the brink of stardom, yet somehow Rourke, in the tiny role of a professional arsonist, stole all the scenes he played with Hurt. 'Mr Kasdan has set out to make a film noir in 1980's [*sic*] clothing', wrote Janet Maslin, who found the transplantation from the 1940s to the 1980s difficult to swallow, because 'without the restrictive social and moral climate of an earlier age, passions can't run as recklessly, dizzyingly high as "Body Heat" says they do. The only places where people still behave as they behave in "Body Heat" are in other movies.'[10] Vincent Canby called it 'a gritty, steamy, amoral and thoroughly satisfying melodrama about adultery, murder and double- and triple-crosses in the kind of seedy Florida cities most tourists fly over', and singled out Rourke for his 'memorable small performance'.[11]

Body Heat was the first of many performances in which Rourke would derive some of his on-screen charisma from his cultivation of the swaggering style of rock music. As Teddy Lewis, the 'rock 'n' roll arsonist', Rourke first nailed the fusion of grit and glitter, flesh and flash that would become his trademark. His costume was the standard Method uniform of T-shirt and jeans, but with the addition of a sparkling diamond earring, aerobic wristband and red hair. He's introduced to the camera as a rock star, mid-musical number, absorbed, sweaty and lip-syncing to Bob Seger's 'I Feel Like a Number' before a nervous audience of one: his lawyer Ned Racine (William Hurt), who has come to his surly young client for some illicit advice on explosives. Teddy Lewis's shop is a windowless dungeon with a bunk bed, the ladder of which he ascends mid-meeting, crawling onto the mattress to lecture to his lawyer from on high, while Racine paces nervously below amidst protruding blades, darts, ropes and tanks of explosives marked with skulls and crossbones. Teddy starts off as the master of the scene, heckling his lawyer for criminal incompetence in a manner both earnest and flamboyant, and affecting a geographically anomalous *Godfather* accent (*Body Heat* is set in Florida). As his musical number about feeling like a number ends, he reaches somewhere off screen to crank the music back up, as though he were in charge of the film's soundtrack. The interest of the scene is Teddy's switch from lording it over Racine to putting himself on the line for him, volunteering to take on the crime 'gratis' and setting himself up for a fall. *Body Heat* associates Rourke (in the film's terms) with the rock music and style of the 1980s, while the other characters are associated with 1940s noir. His loose and casually anachronistic approach to the noir genre typified the way he would blend the culture of the 1950s with the clothing and styles of later periods in *Diner* and *Angel Heart*.

Diner (1982)

Written and directed by Barry Levinson, *Diner* is the first of
Levinson's semi-autobiographical Baltimore series, a set of films
about the city where he grew up that frequently deals with themes of
Jewish assimilation (the series also included 1987's *Tin Cup*, 1990's
Avalon and 1999's *Liberty Heights*). The film, a comedy shot through
with dramatic moments, was a sleeper. It was only because of Pauline
Kael's glowing *New Yorker* review that it was given a wide release at
all. Its excellent ensemble cast included not only Rourke, but also
Ellen Barkin (who, incidentally, had attended the same Miami high
school as Rourke), Kevin Bacon, Steve Guttenberg, Paul Reiser,
Daniel Stern and Timothy Daly, and the film would do much to
launch each of their careers. *Diner* traces the post-adolescent funk of
a group of male friends, all of whom seem lost as to their next moves
in life. They gather at their local diner to hang out, and much of the
film's charm resides in the wit and camaraderie of their banter.
Levinson was nominated for an Academy Award for Best Original
Screenplay. In *The Nation*, Robert Hatch noticed the skill with which
the film walked the line between comedy and drama, sensing that
'these hulking Peter Pans ... play games that at any moment could
turn out to be not so funny', adding that 'only gradually, as you come
to know them better, do you see how the cruelty of their late
childhood is giving way to an appreciation of cause and effect'.[12]
The National Review's John Simon felt that 'These kids are both
ludicrous and pathetic, although the film does not encourage
condescension or beg for sympathy.'[13] Simon also lauded *Diner*'s
realism, and the way that 'The dankness, darkness, drabness of
Baltimore 1959 – and of a certain lower-middle class malaise
anytime, anywhere – are bravely captured here.'

Not only did Rourke become a darling of the influential critic
Pauline Kael with his role as Boogie Sheftell, but he also won the
National Society of Film Critics prize for Best Supporting Actor.

Vincent Canby identified Rourke's performance as the heart of the film (though his screen-time was roughly equal to that of his cast mates), and made the insightful observation that Rourke's physical disposition was that of a boxer:

The focal point of the film is Boogie, played by Mr Rourke who was so memorable in the small but sharply realized role of the arsonist in 'Body Heat.' This is the result of the way the film is written as well as of Mr Rourke's edgily desperate performance as a fellow who is remarkably successful with women but a loser in all other things. Mr Rourke's face tells his story. Even when he's all spruced up in a dinner jacket, as for Eddie's wedding, he always looks as if he were in the ninth round of a boxing match he refuses to admit is lost. It's also to the film's credit that, without any soul-searching whatsoever on Boogie's part, and without any unnecessary exposition, we realize that Boogie understands his situation and may somehow avoid the fate in store.[14]

An important element of the Rourke persona would come into focus in *Diner*: the class difference between Rourke's characters and their love objects (this would become a defining feature of his later softcore roles, which would make working-class men the fetish objects of middle-class women).

In *Diner*, Rourke's cinematic charisma is again developed musically, this time through the voice and persona of Elvis Presley. *Diner* is set in 1959, and each character clings to a different style of identity formation through popular culture: for Eddie (Steve Guttenberg), it's a fixation on the Baltimore Colts. For Shrevie (Daniel Stern), it's a Nick Hornby-style record fetishism. In both cases these intense, boyish attachments are presented as a threat or block to relationships with women. Shrevie fights with his wife Beth when she messes up the order of his catalogue and can't tell the difference between R&B and rock, A-sides and B-sides, and gets angry because she doesn't care that he remembers precisely what song was playing when they met (as though the catalogued version of her in his head is more important than the actual version of her standing in front of him). Eddie refuses to walk down the aisle unless his fiancée passes a Baltimore Colts quiz. Emotions are processed through music in this world, and Levinson's film is reminiscent of *American Graffiti* (1973) in the way that it uses an early rock soundtrack as a shaping force in the characters' lives. It is a film of cruising and radio play. *Diner* establishes its raucous teenage energy immediately: it is set at what looks like a high school dance where Fenwick (Kevin Bacon) is punching holes in a basement window and Boogie is suavely working the room, counselling the guys and brushing off girls to the energetic sounds of 'Shout'. While the nickname of Rourke's character, 'Boogie', is a musical moniker that is never explained, it suitably evokes his playful and slightly jittery character.

The musical culture that forms the background of *Diner* comes to the fore when Guttenberg's Eddie floats a crucial question to the gang: which singer do his friends prefer, 'Sinatra or Mathis?' Eddie is especially curious about what Boogie thinks, because Boogie is cooler than he is. In Eddie's limited musical horizon, he cannot foresee the game-changer with which Boogie answers: 'Presley', a trumping moment that is used to establish Boogie as more rock than his nice-boy friends. While Eddie is debating the merits of which crooner he prefers making out to, Boogie one-ups him by claiming for himself the more flagrant sexuality of rock. When the film ends, all of Boogie's ships seem to have come in, at least temporarily – he's got a rich girl on his arm, his latest gambling debts have dissolved – and in this, his first carefree moment, he touches the jukebox and out pours Elvis singing 'Don't Be Cruel'. It was the first time Presley's estate had licensed one of his tracks for a film he didn't appear in. Soon after, Rourke began preparations for his role as Jerry Lee Lewis in *Great Balls of Fire* (1989), a part that would eventually go to Dennis Quaid. The idea of casting Rourke as Lewis made perfect sense, because even more than Presley, the anarchistic Lewis was a template for Rourke's persona:

exhibitionistic, sexually transgressive, outrageously talented and on a crash course to a premature career flame-out.

Rumble Fish (1983)

Francis Ford Coppola directed *Rumble Fish* hot on the heels of his first S. E. Hinton adaptation, *The Outsiders* (1983), a hit which introduced filmgoers to a generation of new stars including Matt Dillon, Ralph Macchio, Patrick Swayze, Rob Lowe, Emilio Estevez, Tom Cruise and Diane Lane. Some of them returned for *Rumble Fish* (Dillon, Lane) and Coppola introduced some new faces, too, including Rourke and Nicholas Cage. But *Rumble Fish* was not a success in the same league as the earlier film. Whereas the PG-13-rated *Outsiders* grossed $25 million, the R-rated and self-consciously 'arty' *Rumble Fish* lagged far behind at $2.5 million. Critics were divided about the film, and about Coppola's idea of delivering 'an art film for teenagers'.[15] It was filmed in black and white with Expressionist techniques and memorable special effects that emphasised clouds and the graphic patterns left by the shadows of fire escapes. As Motorcycle Boy, Rourke smokes his cigarettes in the manner of a latter-day Camus. Watching the film feels something like witnessing a black-and-white, non-musical sequel to *West Side Story* (1961). Roger Ebert thought it was an experiment worth making, calling *Rumble Fish* 'offbeat, daring, and utterly original',[16] but the film does not stand up to the test of time very well. It never quite transcends the feeling of self-conscious experimentation.

Family guilt is once again a key theme of Rourke's performance. He plays a character, Motorcycle Boy, whose relationships with his alcoholic father and abandoning mother play themselves out in repeated form in his relationship with his younger brother. In Hinton's 1975 young adult novel, the protagonists Rusty

James (played by Matt Dillon) and Motorcycle Boy are fourteen and seventeen years old. Rourke was in his early thirties when he played the role, and so the age of the character was changed to twenty-one (a prematurely aged twenty-one, as other characters in the film note). *Rumble Fish* begins as Motorcycle Boy returns from an absence – a trip to California on a stolen motorcycle – just after Rusty James's friend Steve has warned him, 'You have to face the fact that Motorcycle Boy may be gone for good.' Motorcycle Boy is not so much a realistically drawn character as a mysterious figure at the centre of the story: a teenager's version of Conrad's Kurtz.

In Hinton's novel, the character appears mythically and mysteriously in the middle of a fight, saving his brother: 'I thought we'd stopped this cowboys and Indians crap,' he says, having transcended, in his infinite cool, the need to rumble.[17] Motorcycle Boy's bohemian values are indecipherable in the context of his hometown, and while Hinton's characterisation clearly suggests mental illness, she does not diagnose him, a fact that preserves his mythic nature and also puts us in Rusty James's situation of not understanding the line between his brother's charisma and his pathology:

He had an expressionless face. … He saw things other people couldn't see, and laughed when nothing was funny. He had strange eyes – they made me think of a two-way mirror. Like you could feel somebody on the other side watching you, but the only reflection you saw was your own.[18]

To Rusty James, Motorcycle Boy is sometimes a paternally protective brother, and sometimes an abandoning one. His care comes and goes: like his mother and father, he can never be relied upon.

The alcoholic father in *Rumble Fish* is played by Dennis Hopper (it's exactly the kind of part Rourke might be given today). Hopper is not particularly effective, mainly haunting the sidelines with a hangdog expression. In keeping with the film's themes of inheritance and cycles of dysfunction, Rourke's performance as

Fighting the addictions of his father, *Rumble Fish* (1983)

Motorcycle Boy involves tableaus of attempted resistance to his father's addictions. In a key scene for understanding his Method technique, while Rusty James and a friend talk about him in the background, Rourke as Motorcycle Boy is shown holding his father's bottle to his lips, toying with it, smelling it, touching it to his face, but concertedly not drinking from it. He shakes the bottle, and sets it down. Then he puts a cigarette to his lips and seems to be fighting the urge to light it – the scene ends before we discover if his willpower will hold out. Ultimately, it seems, Motorcycle Boy's father does understand him, but not his own role in creating him. Glamorising his brother's problems as a special fate, his father explains to Rusty that Motorcycle Boy is 'merely miscast in a play. He was born in the wrong era, on the wrong side of the river, with the ability to do anything that he wants to do, and finding nothing that he wants to do. I mean nothing.' Here, we have a return to the dysphoric quality of Rourke's acting – a mismatch between body and role – as well as a commentary on the lack of opportunities presented by his life.

There is something distant and disconnected about *Rumble Fish* as a film, and also about Rourke's performance. This is understandable, since he is portraying a psychologically disturbed character, but it is not quite artistically successful. Janet Maslin noted that 'Mickey Rourke, who plays the Motorcycle Boy, has so much quiet authority that he comes close to making sense of the character, which can't have been easy.'[19] Her use of the word 'close' reminds us that his performance doesn't quite gel. Perhaps it's helpful here to cite Elia Kazan's idea that Method acting performances can sometimes remain too introverted. Kazan thought this was a risk inherent in Method acting technique: 'You see the worst misuse of emotional recall in actors who are really playing with something in themselves – not with the person in the scene. There is this glazed, unconnected look in their eyes, and you know they're somewhere else.'[20] Whether this disconnection was a result of Rourke's over-personalised, over-interiorised preparation, or was simply the right choice to make for a disconnected character, viewers of the film must decide for themselves.

Though Rourke's performance can feel frustratingly inaccessible, it's admirable in its artistic reach, and in *Rumble Fish*, we see evidence that he is not going to inhabit his roles in a 'leading man' style, but will pull his audience in new directions, running the risk of being misunderstood or playing too subtly. In *Body Heat* and *Diner*, Rourke had turned in bold, eye-catching, bravura performances, but in *Rumble Fish*, he went inward and asked viewers to follow him there. His portrayal of Motorcycle Boy in *Rumble Fish* is very different from other high-profile Method-grounded performances of that year, which included Dustin Hoffman's Oscar-nominated turn in *Tootsie* and Paul Newman's in *The Verdict*. In *Rumble Fish*, we see a young actor trying to find his own idiom, while remaining connected to his artistic roots.

The Pope of Greenwich Village (1984)

After inhabiting the role of the abandoned son in *Rumble Fish*, Rourke tried on the part of the failing father in *The Pope of Greenwich Village*. This film, directed by Stuart Rosenberg (of *Cool Hand Luke* [1967] fame), and based on the 1979 novel by Vincent Patrick, tells the story of two cousins – Charlie (Rourke) and Paulie (Eric Roberts). The film follows the lives of these two petty hustlers in New York's restaurant world as they try to pull off a small-time heist. *Pope* is the portrait of the love between two cousins, one of whom has a father (Paulie) and one of whom does not (Charlie). The film ends with the two cousins walking off into the Greenwich Village sunset together – a light riff on 1970s films about New York. Roberts's performance is amusingly mannered, while Rourke, in his scenes with Roberts, is at his most endearing, from his baseball playing to his flirtations with cocktail waitresses to his tender concern for his cousin. Like *Diner*, this is another Rourke film about a boy who can't figure out how to grow up. It's a favourite among his fans, since the young Rourke and Roberts appear to be having such a good time together pretending to be tough guys. If *Rumble Fish* was an art film for the kids, *Pope* was a junior *Mean Streets*.

The film's subplot involves Charlie's relationship with his girlfriend, his ex-wife and his son, with whom he spends occasional custody time. Here, we see intimations of Rourke's future as an on- and off-screen tough guy, and an abrupt end to his sad young man persona of sympathetic identification with women. Here, Rourke veers closer to the 'angry young man'. His character, Charlie Moran, seems very young to be a father, and he is up to his eyeballs in debt. As a father, he's loving when present, but he's not available very often (and is unable to keep up with his child support payments). When his current girlfriend (a dance teacher named Diane, played by Darryl Hannah) announces that she's pregnant, we learn that he doesn't want to become a father again.

Their relationship ends over her desire to keep the baby. In his scenes with Diane, the otherwise likeable Charlie suddenly turns into a jerk. Domestic violence is eroticised, and at the same time the film suggests that the solidarity between two male cousins is much more emotionally gripping than any potential connection between women and men.

As the first phase of his career drew to a close, Rourke's common motifs were coalescing. In terms of role selection, he had a proclivity for street kids, boxers, betting and petty crime, a world of men who are estranged from the women in their lives, and have little else to do but hang out together killing time. As his performance in *Pope* attested, Rourke liked to borrow from the Italian-American tradition, which he came by honestly as an Actors Studio performer who grew up in the shadow of Pacino and De Niro. The film ends with a showdown between Charlie Moran and a local mafia henchman, 'Bed Bug Eddie': this scene shows Rourke claiming the title of Little Italy's new 'pope'. His campy and affectionate inhabitance of this macho mafia role was sometimes endearing, but as the sad young man aged, he found himself increasingly pushed beyond the fluidity and flexibility of his early persona, and subject to greater pressures of masculine conformity. There began to emerge an arrogant, misogynist side of Rourke's persona: soon he would be slinging racial slurs at his lover in *Year of the Dragon*. This new side of Rourke comes out unmistakably in a scene at the midpoint of *The Pope of Greenwich Village*. Charlie is fighting with Diane in a stairwell. His planned heist has exposed her to danger. She slaps him. 'Hit me again, see if I change,' he challenges her. He grabs her arm violently. And then, he gives her a last look with his matinee idol's eyes – blinking, wet with tears, expressive – before taking them away for ever. He flicks up the collar of his leather jacket, carefully places his dark 1980s sunglasses over his eyes, smiles what Cintra Wilson would call his 'fuck you smile', and walks away from her for good.[21] It was a clear on-screen announcement that Rourke was cutting himself off from those performances of emotional openness, empathy with women and sad young manhood that had brought him to Hollywood notice, and was heading for a rockier, more dangerous future.

2 SOFTCORE STAR

The more remote that I became, the more they liked it.

James Wheeler, *Wild Orchid*

In the glittering, moneyed Hollywood of the 1980s, Rourke hit the big time, taking risks in his choice of roles and turning in a few inspiring performances. But the broad arc of his career through this decade was a downward one. By the end of the 1980s, the contradictions of his star image had brought about a personal crisis that sent Rourke spiralling out of Hollywood. As we have seen, his breakthrough came with a series of rebel-inflected roles in Lawrence Kasdan's *Body Heat*, Barry Levinson's *Diner* and Francis Ford Coppola's *Rumble Fish*. As a latter-day James Dean or Montgomery Clift, he played parentless working-class youths with poetical souls who forged intimate but fragile relationships. His persona was particularly appealing to women, for whom it seemed to offer a bridge to the modes of freedom and rebellion he embodied. 'I like his insolence,' said French actress Fanny Ardant, 'he throws himself in all directions, he reminds me of Brando when he was young.'[1] The early Rourke fused recklessness and tenderness, extending the promise of some intangibly subversive and lyrical coolness. In his first major roles he played the hoodlum as rent boy, always making himself sexually available to the camera. But though he worked in a post-*Midnight Cowboy* world, Rourke always closeted his hustlers, displacing the signifiers of gay male

'Towering, claustrophobic, and exhausting':
Cimino's *Year of the Dragon* (1985)

sexuality onto a series of other risky businesses. Like Brando, Dean
and Paul Newman before him, he turned the figure of the hustler
toward women. He became known for his seductive whispering.

He made a notable leap from this early lost-boy persona to a
more aggressive, 1970s style of Method masculinity when he landed
the role of Stanley White in Michael Cimino's *Year of the Dragon*,
a clean-up-the-streets cop epic set in New York's Chinatown. But the
1970s were over, and Cimino's style struck critics as 'towering,
claustrophobic, and exhausting'.[2] Rourke's acting seemed a bit like
that too. As Stanley White, Rourke had dyed his hair grey to play a
character nearly twenty years his senior and seemed out of his depth.
Next, he turned down a series of hotshot roles in films like *Rain Man*
and *Top Gun* to explore the seedier, anti-hero terrain of erotic and
suspense thrillers.

At the peak of his Hollywood fame, Rourke specialised in
sleaze. This aspect was there from the start, but it became a more

'The sleaziest and most charismatic of the bunch': Barry Levinson's *Diner* (1982)

and more significant part of his persona. If in *Diner* Rourke played the sleazy element in a respectable film, by the time he made the straight-to-video sequel to *9½ Weeks* (*Love in Paris*) in 1997, Rourke was the only (and scarcely) respectable element in a decidedly sleazy film. In *9½ Weeks*, he somehow met in the middle. This was the classic but fleeting mid-1980s Rourke image: a handsome movie star, a good actor and an incarnation of the zeitgeist. Despite the hits he took for acting in such a 'woman's' film, in *9½ Weeks* Rourke just about struck a balance between movie stardom and a proclivity for sleazy roles. But sleaze usually won the day. Beginning with Kael's designation of Boogie Sheftell as 'the sleaziest and most charismatic of the bunch' in *Diner*, it's a word that's never far from the lips of anyone responding to Rourke's persona.[3] He nearly stole *Body Heat* as a 'sleazy arsonist';[4] *9½ Weeks* was 'the film that pushed Rourke towards ... sleazy sex';[5] 'sleazy, greasy Mickey Rourke finally takes a bath. But it's a bloodbath,' was one critic's verdict on *Angel Heart*;[6]

he was lauded for his 'resplendently sleazy performance as Charles Bukowski' in *Barfly*;[7] *Wild Orchid* is 'a miserably stupid and sleazy wank film';[8] and in a comeback cameo in *The Rainmaker*, he was scene-stealing as 'sleazy lawyer Bruiser Stone'.[9] The least pejorative meaning of the word is shabbiness: sleaze as a condition of dilapidation or physical dirtiness. A Rourke character usually meets this basic standard. He lives in squalor for any number of reasons – poverty, alcoholism, self-loathing, bohemian spirit or sheer lack of will to live – but without a failure of hygiene there would be no Mickey Rourke film persona. His characters sleep in motels and boarding houses, chain-smoke, drink straight from the bottle and eat off other people's plates. They patch the rips in their clothes with duct tape. They also inhabit landscapes of sleaze, the places where people go to be thrilled and amused, to gamble, have sex and get high. And they are not just passing through: they make their lives amidst the marginal, transient souls who inhabit such communities. They identify more completely with the sleazy world than the respectable one. In *Barfly*, as Henry Chinaski, Rourke moves between a crummy rented room and a crummy bar. In *A Prayer for the Dying* (1987), his character hides out in a brothel. Motorcycle Boy in *Rumble Fish* frequents dances and pool halls on the wrong side of the river. And in *The Wrestler*, Randy the Ram lives in a trailer park and hangs out in strip clubs and on the deserted boardwalks of the New Jersey shore. Rourke's characters' commitment to the world of attractions is not just a romantic solidarity of outsiderdom: they live among the attractions because they are attractions too. The vulgar cultural products of sleaze – pornography, fighting and gambling – relate to the viewer in a particular way, seeming to promise a kind of visceral satisfaction. They have a service function. And so does Rourke, whose performances continually inhabit the uncertain space between acting and the sex trade.

But his characters are not 'sleazy' in the way you might think. The classic male sleaze is a predator, acting narcissistically on his

Sleazy landscapes: Harry Angel at Coney
Island in Alan Parker's *Angel Heart* (1987)

own desire, reducing other people to objects. On the surface, Rourke
gives this impression. His characters sport the right jewellery and
know the right lines. But he always plays against the grain of a sleazy
scene, emerging as a misunderstood gentleman who finds himself in
a sleazy situation for a sweet reason. As Boogie in *Diner*, Rourke
perfected the technique. His smirk is always at the ready, and he's a
little too good at talking his way out of whatever hot water he's gotten
into. 'I'll take all the action I can get', he says, but when push comes
to shove, he won't sell anyone out to make a buck. When it counts,
he turns from lover to protective friend. This is clearest in his half-
seduction of Beth (Ellen Barkin), an old flame who reconnects with
Boogie in a moment of weakness. Beth needs a self-esteem boost
after a fight with her husband, while Boogie needs a girl he can pass
off as his date to win a bet. Boogie's lines to his married ex-girlfriend
are rarified sleaze – 'I often think of the nights we spent together',
'you're a very sexy lady', 'I think we should get together' – but he
plays against them to complicate the scene. His come-ons are
troubled by reluctance, kindness and a worried gaze, and we get the

impression that he's chatting her up for her benefit, not his.
Sleaze becomes chivalry. This is confirmed later that night when
Boogie gets her halfway up the stairs to the bedroom, and then
decides that her well-being is more important than winning his bet.
He calls off the liaison: 'bet or no bet, it's not right,' he mumbles.
Now he shifts into his most comfortable role of relationship
counsellor. 'You and Shrevie should work your thing out,' he tells
her. 'I think it would be worth it.' Seducing to the point where
conquest is certain and then calling off the seduction is Boogie's
signature move. The key to his charm is that he doesn't exploit, even
though he can. He combines intense emotional availability with
absolute sexual unavailability. Much later, in *The Wrestler*, Rourke
would again play a character who is caught up in sleazy situations for
sentimental reasons: for instance, Randy just wants to have a
heart-to-heart chat with the exotic dancer Cassidy (Marisa Tomei),
but he ends up having to buy a lap dance to get one. They both
ignore the fact that she's gyrating naked on his knees while they
gossip about their lives. What distinguishes him from a real sleaze is
his motivation. The question of his pleasure isn't even on the table.

It's the kick Rourke's characters seem to get from taking
someone for a ride, rather than the sleaziness of exploitation, that's
most characteristic of his persona. There's nothing in it for the
characters he plays except a kind of vicarious pleasure in the pleasure
of the other. In a moment of kinesthetic catharsis in *Rumble Fish*,
Motorcycle Boy takes his brother out for a high-risk ride through the
deserted city streets. Colour blind and half-deaf, he seems to be
ferrying his brother into some other realm, and they avoid crashing
by the skin of their teeth. From film to film, Rourke's stoic characters
orchestrate the pleasure of the other, a pleasure that fascinates,
baffles and enchants. More gigolo than sleazeball, he projects an aura
of availability and exclusivity that Kael picked up on when she noted
that Rourke in *Diner* is 'the most tender in his dealings with women,
and the most gallant', and that he found a way to extend that

gallantry into the darkened cinema, with 'an edge and a magnetism … He seems to be acting to you, and to no one else.'[10]

He would find the perfect outlet for such talents in *9½ Weeks* (1986). If you grew up in the 1980s and 1990s, then this was the kind of movie you only caught quick glimpses of on television before your parents changed the channel. Lyne's characters dress like real grown-ups, with an elegance of costume rare in films then or now – classic tailoring, neutral tones, pumps, pearls, trench coats. Rourke and Basinger look far less dated in *9½ Weeks* than many of their cinematic counterparts of that year. As softcore, the film was subject to the complex critical fortunes of that genre, which, as Linda Williams notes, tends to be 'disparaged both as a sex film manqué (not explicit enough) and yet still as a kind of pornography for women'.[11] Critics mostly veered toward the former, faulting the film for stopping short rather than going too far: the handcuffs and riding crops that characterise sadomasochistic subculture persist only in 'cutesy residue', complained Sheila Benson, who found Lyne's treatment 'sanitizing'.[12] Others followed suit: 'juvenile and sentimental';[13] 'vacuous';[14] 'pricelessly funny without having many laughs';[15] 'the pity is that there are elements here for a very edgy, very adult melodrama'.[16] The general tone of these comments can be attributed to the anti-softcore prejudice, but there was another reason for the feeling that the film had been sanitised. In order to qualify for an R (rather than X) rating, and in response to Los Angeles screenings at which audiences reacted negatively, Lyne had cut several major scenes, including one in which Rourke's character induced Basinger's to commit suicide with him by taking pills, only to reveal after she had swallowed them that they were sugar pills. A less dramatically cut version, screened in Europe, fared well, playing in Paris theatres for a year. Because of the ratings and screen-test concerns, the American version looked, as Vincent Canby put it, as if it had been 'edited with a pair of garden shears'.[17] Canby also complained about the film's saturation in fashion and commodity culture, suggesting that 'John … carries his beautifully cut, expensive suits so well that he becomes their accessory', and that this was '*The Story of O* as it might look if conceived as a two-hour television commercial' (Canby also teased Rourke's male model stubble).[18] Sheila Benson, too, noted Lyne's 'fashion photographer's eye', and Mark Morris of *The Observer* sensed that 'Lyne's true passion was for the matt black surfaces that defined Mickey Rourke's existence'.[19]

Who could blame critics for laughing at the film's pared-down, pseudo-profound dialogue and (except in the musical sequences) total absence of levity about sex? But most grudgingly conceded that there was something more to Lyne's enterprise than 'a pair of chic Manhattanites playing with pain',[20] and that the 'more' mostly came from Rourke's performance: 'There's something calculating and dangerous about Rourke who has never looked more attractive. He plays John as charming, but frighteningly secretive';[21] 'Basinger is fine, but it is Rourke who makes the film work … Rourke keeps it plausible that it's more likely that John's heart will be broken than Elizabeth's';[22] 'in a richly satisfying performance, John is mysterious and hypnotic; at once cruel and tender, giving and taking';[23] 'Rourke is perfectly cast as the borderline psychopath';[24] 'Rourke [is] boyishly charming, with a sort of All-American handsomeness … John remains a question mark';[25] Rourke's 'animal magnetism and hooded sleaziness is ideal for John, a character conceived with care … we can feel in Rourke's energy (it's a remarkable performance) the psychological block he faces when he at last attempts to see women as more than dolls who need alternately to be fed and spanked'.[26]

The mid-1980s was not a fortuitous time for a sex film. Amidst the puritanical climate of the Reagan years, the AIDS crisis and the movement by some feminists toward an alliance with conservative groups to promote the censorship of pornography, it was hard for just about anyone in America to admit they liked *9½*

Weeks.[27] But despite the film's unpopularity with feminist audiences, David Andrews claims in *Soft in the Middle: The Contemporary Softcore Feature in Its Contexts* that '9½ *Weeks* can be read as a woman's film, opening with Elizabeth ... walking towards the camera through crowded streets, and ending with her walking away from it', and that it tells the story from Elizabeth's point of view, moving her 'from the position of a confused divorcee to that of a woman in control of her choices'.[28] Nonetheless, North American critics more frequently saw 9½ *Weeks* as a cry for help: 'What Elizabeth needs is a self-help book with the title "Why Nice Women Date Creeps".'[29] For many viewers in 1986, 9½ *Weeks* read as a regressive film about a woman psychologically held hostage by a man, not one about a woman who had embarked on a consensual relationship involving the dynamics of domination and submission. In the media, Kim Basinger confirmed this interpretation by describing the emotional stress she faced while filming it, as Rourke's and Lyne's acting and directing techniques seemed to duplicate far too closely for comfort the humiliation and domination that Basinger's character experienced. In an interview in the *Toronto Star*, Basinger said of beginning work on the film, 'I met with Mickey, which was one of the worst days I've lived through', and then described the off-screen manipulations designed to make her feel as uncomfortable as possible on set, in the hopes that such treatment would facilitate her performance.[30] Lyne's techniques included barring her from off-screen contact with Rourke in order to make her feel more in tune with her character. Basinger was not included in discussions about whether these techniques would be helpful for her, and Lyne made patronising comments to the media about her lack of intellect and grasp of the film's themes. Basinger's account suggests that whether we choose to classify it as a 'woman's film' or not, the ethics governing the making of 9½ *Weeks* were anything but feminist.

On screen, however, both Rourke and Basinger share the conventional woman's role of erotic pleasure-giver and object of the gaze. *9½ Weeks* is most transparent in its handling of Rourke as male courtesan. Here he's not the Christopher Street hustler but his Wall Street counterpart, the arbitrageur who looks like a catalogue model. He seduces the disaffected divorcee Elizabeth with steady eye contact in New York's Chinatown and an outdoor market full of antiques. He wraps her in a luxurious wished-for scarf, seemingly pulled from nowhere. 'Your business is very risky, isn't it?' a tantalised Elizabeth asks, and he offers up the pleasure of danger to her in return: 'Well, it's not any riskier than you coming here ... I mean we hardly know each other,' a threat that's belied by his almost-teasing tone, and the fact that he's batting his eyelashes. The pleasure is all hers, the expressions of danger part of the performance. He becomes her lover, father and the child she never had. At the street market, she delights in a wind-up chicken that lays wooden eggs, bargaining it down to a price she can afford just as John appears on the scene, a mischievous man-child who gets caught up in silly bets with kids on the boardwalk. But at home, this child transforms into a father when he brushes her hair and airplanes spoonfuls of soup into her mouth. While Elizabeth is hypnotised and multi-orgasmic, John remains vigilant. Giving her thrills is a full-time job. He wakes up before Elizabeth, lays out her clothes, feeds her breakfast in bed, puts in a gruelling day on Wall Street, then comes home, showers her with lingerie, cooks dinner and stage-manages erotic adventures. In the memorable (and much parodied) scene which features a blindfolded Elizabeth in front of an open fridge being fed strawberries, chilli peppers, olives and cough syrup to the wholesome music of The Newbeats's 'I Like Bread and Butter', she relaxes into abandon, kicking her honey-drenched legs with delight, while John approaches his role as an artist of sensation half-scientifically, half in jest. To make sure he seduces the audience as thoroughly as he does Elizabeth, Rourke and Lyne recycle all the tricks from Valentino's woman-pleaser *The Sheik* (1921): the rebuff of covering up a naked woman after she has willingly disrobed; the summoning claps and hand gestures; cigarettes louchely dangling from the mouth; rituals of dressing and undressing; breaks in the plot to focus on the erotic contemplation of his face and body; the creative use of perspective to subvert moments of supposed genital congress; the coy introduction of handcuffs and whips that are never used in the ways you expect.[31]

Lyne's film replaces the more classically sadomasochistic dynamics of the original 1978 memoir by Elizabeth McNeill with something more like two masochists in search of a sadist.[32] 'How did you know I'd respond to you the way I have?' a mystified Elizabeth asks John at the film's midpoint. He answers, with no elaboration, 'Because I saw myself in you.' As Rourke plays John, his inhabitance of the sadist's part is all a terrible misunderstanding, or perhaps a temporary agreement. Longingly toying with Elizabeth's stockings, urging her into men's suits, John does everything in his power *not* to play the role while still superficially filling it. He only gets to have fun twice, first during the kitchen floor food scene, and then when Elizabeth is discovering the pleasures of striptease to Joe Cocker's 'You Can Leave Your Hat On'. These two musical moments allow Rourke to do what he does best: portray the enjoyment of another person's enjoyment. It's a tough acting assignment, to watch a woman strip in an uncreepy way. Basinger and Rourke play this scene masterfully. She comes fully out of her shell for the first time, and he, eyes alight with enchantment, sits barefoot on the floor with a bowl of popcorn and a cigarette, sliding ever downward until he's lying at her feet.

In the first half of *9½ Weeks*, John is endowed with the trappings of the pirate and the magician: planks, white sheets that he spreads out with a dramatic flourish, strange chairs that see-saw, smooth fabrics, glass jars that refract, wristwatches that hypnotise. The second half of the film encodes what lies beneath this enchanted surface. Lyne communicates the violent eroticism of John's character with a few none-too-subtle visual reminders, like mice dangling from the mouths of cats, fish flipping around on dry land and paintings of

Adrian Lyne's *9½ Weeks* (1986). Basinger
performs … Rourke observes

dog collars. But Rourke approaches John's menace through gesture, condensing it into brief, cryptic physical movements: the ripping off of a belt, the punching of a table, the testing of a whip against the air. Not chewing the scenery so much as doing gymnastics with it, Rourke brings to the role an art of leverage, pushing off against solid objects in a way that borrows their force and directs it against Elizabeth. As they make love in a clock tower, he braces his hands against a wall, as though it were a springboard. Then in a rain-filled gutter, he places them on top of her head and pulls down, as though trying to pull her further into him.

In return for his attempts to incorporate Elizabeth, to take over her body, he offers her masculine privilege and hints at his own willingness to renounce it. A shared understanding of gender as performance informs the striptease and cross-dressing scenes of *9½ Weeks*. Rather than upholding the distinction between male gaze and female body, John in the striptease scene undermines it by becoming the pedagogue, one who doesn't passively consume the spectacle but helps to create it, teaching Elizabeth with choreographic gestures how to strip, and suggesting his own girlish embarrassment as he lowers his head and covers his eyes when she attains a professional's level of shamelessness. Earlier in the film, he buys her a man's suit, meets her at the bar of the Algonquin Hotel, hands her brandy and a cigar, and tells her all about life on the other side, ending the evening by asking, 'So what do you want to do? Pick up some chicks?' John relates to her as an honorary male and invites her to share the pleasures of sleaze. Rourke's defining 1980s performances let women in on the moment of perversity. The popcorn scene in *Diner* has that charge, too, when his post-adolescent prankster pulls off the kind of stunt of which teen sex comedies are made: smirking at friends while flashing a girl at the movies. If it ended there, it would just be annoying. What makes the scene interesting is that Boogie follows his date out of the darkened theatre and into the women's bathroom, where he proceeds to explain the whole thing, transforming her from

John takes Elizabeth on a tour of masculinity in
Adrian Lyne's *9½ Weeks* (1986)

the butt of the joke into a co-conspirator. In the sexually segregated
world of 1950s Baltimore, he becomes a native informant who
explains to her the workings of the hard-on.

As the 1980s progressed, Rourke's erotic persona turned
nihilist, decadent, existential. *9½ Weeks*, *Angel Heart* and *Barfly* made
French audiences fall in love with him as he revealed himself to be an
athlete of the heart with a compulsion for underworlds and depths of
experience. As though the blood of Baudelaire and Artaud coursed
through his veins, he drank out of fire hydrants and wallowed in
pools of filth and blood-drenched rain. He gained a cult following:
a tour through the archives turns up admiring writing about Rourke
in every genre. In *The New York Times*, Alessandra Stanley wrote a
loving tribute through the eyes of Rourke's rabid French fan base,
explaining how in Paris, 'his name is pronounced reverently' and
women go mad for 'Le Look Rourke, a state of fashionable abandon
– faded jeans, dirty hair, two-day stubble'.[33] From smitten
reminiscences by Charles Bukowski to a prize-winning poem called
'After an Evening with Mickey Rourke I Pick up Petrarch' (about a

narrator left so feverish by *Year of the Dragon* that she has to read sonnets 'to distract me from my tetched romantic bent; an overdose of romance usually cures it'), Rourke inspired a torrent of passionate adulation.[34] From 1981 to 1987, he was a kind of erotic hypnotist. Perhaps what made fans need to keep looking at him was a face that didn't add up: charm and despair, insouciance and submission, incomprehension and insight. His eyes spoke plainly of knowing something awful, and he assumed protectiveness over others while having no idea how to protect himself.

9½ Weeks was a timely film in its preoccupation with the glamour and depravity of the 1980s, and it made both Rourke and Basinger into global sex symbols. But it spelled a notable change in the perception of Rourke: he began a critical descent in Hollywood, from a serious and exciting young actor to a tawdry woman's star.[35] And it was not the misogyny or sadism in Rourke's persona but the masochism and femininity that caused the most discomfort with his new role as the purveyor of softcore pleasure. When Rourke turned from acting to boxing at the end of the decade, it was because he had started to regard acting as a 'career for sissies'.[36] That's a long-standing anti-theatrical, misogynist and homophobic platitude. But, as the reviews of *9½ Weeks* mocking his 'model's appearance' suggest, Rourke wasn't just being paranoid: his acting *was* being feminised in pejorative ways. In the films in which women responded so strongly to him, it is important to recognise that this was because he took up a woman's position, both visually and in terms of the plot. His performances complicated film theorist Laura Mulvey's thesis about the economy of the gaze (Mulvey argued in her classic 1975 essay 'Visual Pleasure and Narrative Cinema' that cinema is premised on the idea of a heterosexual male viewer taking pleasure in the female body). Rourke's films, frequently positioning him as the object of mystery and desire, as the body to be known and made responsive, were geared toward a heterosexual female or gay male gaze. At a certain point, after having accepted such film roles

The purveyor of softcore pleasures: Rourke
and Otis in Zalman King's *Wild Orchid* (1990)

instead of the more conventionally 'manly' ones he'd also been
offered, he seemed to fall prey to the psychic and professional
pressures of objectification.

If Rourke had only made films like Lyne's *9½ Weeks* and
Parker's *Angel Heart*, which were erotic but with legitimate directors
and co-stars, he might have been able to pull off something like the
career of Michael Douglas between *Fatal Attraction* and *Disclosure*
(seedy, but recoverable). But he went too far with *Wild Orchid*
(1990), casting the Guess model Carré Otis as his co-star, and
debuting a new tanned and muscled appearance. If, as Susan Sontag
suggested with an allusion to Genet, there's 'a good taste of bad
taste', then *Wild Orchid* wasn't it.[37] The film's script was so low
quality, its acting so poor and its depiction of Brazil as a land of
erotic awakening so earnest that it seems challenging even to reclaim
it as camp. It was at this point that a perception of Rourke's
sleaziness definitively overtook his hard-earned artistic credibility.

In what follows, I will take a closer look at some of Rourke's films from this height-of-career moment that so quickly turned into his descent and exile from Hollywood.

Angel Heart (1987)

Set in 1955, and based on the novel *Falling Angel* by William Hjortsberg (1978), Alan Parker's *Angel Heart* tells the story of Harry Angel, a private detective hired to trace a crooner who disappeared after sustaining major injuries in the Second World War. Critics were confused by the film's hybrid genre. 'An odd, utterly humorless fusion of private-eye melodrama and occult-horror film,' judged Vincent Canby in *The New York Times*, with a 'murky, pointless narrative' and a protagonist (Rourke) who 'displays the persistence of a very dim door-to-door salesman who's the last one to know that he has no knack for the job'.[38] Roger Ebert was a bit kinder, detecting in the film 'a sly sense of humor, good acting and directing' and suggesting that, in his performance as the devil in this Faust variation, Robert De Niro was parodying his own Mephistopheles, Martin Scorsese.[39] It's 'the perfect cult movie', predicted Rita Kempley of *The Washington Post*, who called Rourke 'one of Hollywood's up-and-coming career degenerates' and judged him to be 'at his rancid best'.[40] The plot is too tortuous for a précis. How did Johnny Liebling become Johnny Favorite and then Harry Angel? It's not terribly clear – apparently not even to the film's actors. Angel's investigation takes him to Louisiana, where he gets a glimpse of Southern life in the early civil rights era. Here, it seems, the British director Parker is conducting a dress rehearsal for his next film, *Mississippi Burning* (1988).[41] In that work, Parker's problematic race politics received the level of scrutiny they deserved, but with *Angel Heart*, the media focused on the underage Lisa Bonet's appearance as Rourke's love interest. *Angel Heart* is a film that is uncertain how to represent race, or rather, how to pay lip service to liberal sentiments while still using crude Hollywood stereotypes of vodou as an aesthetic canvas for the sexual debauchery of the white protagonist. *Angel Heart* tries half-heartedly to register the importance of its setting by showing Harry Angel, with his underdog sensibilities, taking a seat in a 'Colored' section on the bus, anticipating a similar scene in *Mississippi Burning*, but this historical backdrop is not seriously explored.

As Harry Angel, Rourke riffs on hard-boiled protagonists like Sam Spade and Philip Marlowe (in a scene featuring an actual hard-boiled egg, Parker seems to be having some postmodern fun with the genre). Clearly enjoying the opportunity to embrace the cinematic heritages of the detective genre, Rourke endows Angel with a scar, a limp, a strong Brooklyn accent and, to show just how hardened he is, he strikes up a match using the shoe of his latest victim. Rourke often embellishes the edges of even his toughest characters with a childish sweetness, and here it emerges in an early scene of the film as Angel heads out onto the streets of the city smoking a cigarette while also blowing pink bubbles with his gum. The story is a Jekyll and Hyde variation: Rourke must play both the hapless private detective Harry Angel, and also, in glimpses, the murderous charismatic Johnny Favorite. His acting is at its most intense and meaty in the scene following the revelation that the two men are in fact one, that Harry Angel *is* Johnny Favorite, and that he has had sex with and then murdered his own daughter. The script calls for Rourke to repeat the line 'I know who I am' several times, and on each occasion his level of panic and uncertainty about this sentiment escalates. It's a vigorous piece of acting, and one that would probably have had greater impact in a better film.

In assessing his first performance since *9½ Weeks*, critics seemed interested in codifying Rourke's transforming star image. Canby weighs his previous impression against what he finds to be Rourke's underwhelming appearance in this film:

With the right role, Mr Rourke is a good, interesting, vivid actor. Here he's suitably intense, but to such little effect you're likely to note that as 1955's Harry Angel, he sports the same two-day-old, male-model stubble (and 'Miami Vice' wardrobe) he used for his 1986 character in '9½ Weeks.'[42]

Rourke's talent was still apparent to Roger Ebert, who writes that 'Rourke occupies the center of the film like a violent unmade bed. No other actor, with the possible exception of France's Gerald [sic] Depardieu, has made such a career out of being a slob. He looks unshaven, unwashed, hung over and desperate.'[43] The scenes with De Niro remind us that Rourke in this period was drifting in search of his own Scorsese, while the episodes with fortune-teller character Charlotte Rampling (of Cavani's *The Night Porter* [1974] fame) remind us that he was as drawn to the role of the kink diva as to that of the intense Method actor.

Angel Heart, like *9½ Weeks*, is a film of graphic sexuality, but it inhabits the register of suspense rather than softcore. When Harry Angel enquires about Johnny Favorite (himself), he hears that he was known for two things: 'My mother said he was about as close to true evil as she ever wanted to come' and 'he was a terrific lover'. The complex demands of memory and forgetfulness in the plot make it hard to get any sense of Rourke's character, other than his confusion. Detective Harry Angel's sexual persona mostly seems goofy – he flirts with women to facilitate his investigations. But in the brief glimpses of Johnny Favorite through Harry Angel, we see his 'true evil' in the Sweeney Todd savouring of a murder committed with a long razor blade, and in the way Rourke attacks a block of ice. His sexuality becomes most horrifying in the film's final scene. He begins interrogating Bonet's character Epiphany Proudfoot about her personal life in his rundown hotel room: 'Seventeen ... that's kind of young to have a kid, isn't it?', to which Bonet responds, 'It's old enough.' Epiphany is a stereotype of free Southern sexuality. They dance. One thing leads to another. But the tone changes from sultry to horrifying when we begin to notice that the rain leaking through the roof is actually blood. Here the scene transforms into a violent, murderous orgy, as Harry Angel is overtaken by Johnny Favorite and slaughters his lover. The violent sex scene with Bonet encapsulates Rourke's erotic persona in all its dimensions: his allure is often predicated on a racist primitivism (in *9½ Weeks*, he seduces Elizabeth to the sounds of Billie Holiday's 'Strange Fruit'); his desire conflates generations and gender; his sexuality is defined by violence; and sexual identity is figured as a tortuous negotiation of identity and desire, often characterised by the fear of the exposure of some horrifying truth through sex. In Rouke's films of the mid-to-late 1980s, sex is a powerful act of intimacy that has the power to shatter the self. Intensely romantic notions of women exist side by side with misogyny and an inability actually to live with them on a day-to-day basis. 'Secret loves should stay secret', Angel says romantically early in the film, but *Angel Heart* ultimately works to show that psychic dissolution is the price of such closeting.

From this hard-boiled neo-noir spiked with horror that wasn't clearly a hit or a miss, Rourke went on to make another interesting choice, this time working with a French director on a small budget.

Barfly (1987)

'An unshaven Mickey Rourke delivers his lines like W. C. Fields and swaggers like a gutter prince', wrote Jonathan Rosenbaum about *Barfly*.[44] With a screenplay by Charles Bukowski, confident direction by Barbet Schroeder (known for his films about addicts and street denizens) and a truly engaging performance by Rourke, *Barfly* is a hidden gem of the 1980s. It's set along the Sunset Strip at the height of its cultural energy as the home of the hair metal scene. But that world isn't the one protagonist Harry Chinaski (based on Bukowski) inhabits – instead, his is the world of the old LA bars. And sex isn't the only, or by any means the most important, pleasure of *Barfly*. The plot is focused on Chinaski's perpetual quest to bum drinks from reluctant bartenders. Beyond that, he spends his time getting into bar fights, listening to classical music on the radio and writing late into the night. He is not picky about women, though they seem to be drawn to him for his tolerance and easygoing nature, as well as for his bohemian splendour. Without thinking very hard about it (all he says is 'she looks OK'), he falls into a relationship with an older, down-on-her-luck woman, a fellow barfly named Wanda (played by Faye Dunaway). She has a frail body and even frailer self-esteem, and is haunted by nightmares of impending death. He moves into her apartment, and though their first loyalties are both elsewhere (hers to booze, his to writing), they experiment with the possibility that they might learn to be faithful to each other.

The rival love interest in the film is played by a posh literary editor named Tully Sorenson (Alice Krige) who has taken an interest in Chinaski's writing. To locate him as he floats between cheap rented rooms, she hires a private detective, and when she first appears at his door with a cheque to pay for the piece she's accepted for publication, he thinks she's from a collection agency. During her visit, she witnesses some of the Chinaski lifestyle – mid-conversation, he goes over to a neighbour's apartment to break up what he thinks is an incident of domestic violence (and which may actually be an SM scene), ends up stabbing a guy, calls a paramedic, then returns to his conversation with Tully. As is usual in Rourke films, she is more interested in him than he is in her. In a long drive up to her luxurious house in the Hollywood Hills, she tries to seduce him into her world of privilege. When she goes into a bank to cash the cheque she's offered him, he moves into the driver's seat of her convertible, test-driving what it would be like to live out the 1980s-style wealth and glamour she represents. It's not long before he learns the perils of the fast life driving down the Sunset Strip in LA, as, irritated by the driver in front of him, he starts honking and calling him names, then jumps out of the car and starts a scene. While most of the film's location shots feature seedier parts of the Strip, this one takes place in the very heart of the entertainment scene, in front of the Chateau Marmont (and as though Schroeder is commenting on Hollywood's priorities, a giant billboard for *Spaceballs* fills the background).

Chinaski's inability to show reverence for wealth becomes even more pronounced when he reaches Tully's house. The first thing he does is don a ridiculous pair of sunglasses with palm trees on the sides. She offers him a drink, and then she offers him a comfortable place to live and write, but he can't bear the thought of being a kept man. He sees her comfortable lifestyle as 'a cage with golden bars'. In such moments, Rourke seems to have worked out a clever solution to delivering Chinaski's more obnoxious and existentially profound lines – he drawls, speaks slowly, gestures elaborately and always sounds a bit like he's kidding. The two get drunk and inevitably end up in bed. But when they wake up in the morning, he proves as impervious to feelings of male honour as he did to offers of money. He kisses Tully and heads for the door, happy to be returning to his street life and Wanda. She is enraged and he explains himself as simply as he can: 'I didn't want anything ugly to happen.' His free-love ethos returns at the end of the film when Tully and Wanda get into a barfight over him. To subdue the situation, he philosophises: 'There's no reality to any of this', as if he's trying to reason with insane people. And insane they might be, to want a piece of this drunken dime-store philosopher who always seems to have a bloody lip from his latest fight, and who spends most of his time with greasy hair falling in his face, wearing a too-small white T-shirt and a saggy pair of boxer shorts.

Somehow, Rourke pulls this off: his Chinaski is, against all odds, a charmer. He delivers the character's bitter beat lines with an earnest confusion that becomes comic ('Sometimes I just get tired of thinking of all the things that I don't wanna do. All the things that I don't wanna be. Places I don't wanna go, like India, like getting my

'To my friends!': Rourke as Henry Chinaski in
Barbet Schroeder's *Barfly* (1987)

teeth cleaned. Save the whale, all that, I don't understand that').
As Chinaski, Rourke walks like he's pregnant, with his feet spread
wide apart and his back arched. In addition to observing Bukowski
on the set, it also looks like Rourke might have done some animal
exercises to develop the physical identity of his character: there's
something positively feral about his movements when he jumps
over the bar and starts drinking beer straight from the tap.
Rourke exaggerates Bukowksi's mannerisms to create an even more
eccentric and memorable character. In his subsequent novel,
Hollywood, based on the filming process, Bukowski writes approvingly
about Rourke (under the name of 'Jack Bledsoe'): 'The door to the
room opened and Jack Bledsoe weaved in. Shit, it was the young
Chinaski! It was me! I felt a tender aching within me.'[45]

Actors sometimes rely on recurring physical gestures which
serve as a sort of shorthand for their characters, and here Rourke

demonstrates a few of them. One is holding his hands out in a beseeching manner that seems to indicate many things: the clown waiting for applause, the beggar looking for a handout, the philosopher giving up on finding an answer. *Barfly* has a different sexual sensibility than most of Rourke's films – it is decidedly less tortured about heterosexuality, monogamy and a man's sexual performance. When Chinaski applies for a job and is asked for his sex, he says 'you can put male if you like'. When Wanda goes home with the bartender Eddie (played by Frank Stallone), Chinaski objects because 'he stands for everything I despise: Obviousness. Unoriginal, macho energy. Ladies' man.' But Rourke was about to enter the period of his career during which he most urgently felt the need to assert the very kind of muscular, over-the-top manhood that his character Chinaski dismisses.

This change of style was accompanied by, and related to, changes in Rourke's appearance. In 1989, he made *Johnny Handsome* with director Walter Hill. A study of disability and criminality, the part was seemingly a deviation from the sexy roles he was accumulating, but the core issues remained the same. Rourke played the role of a disfigured criminal who is given plastic surgery by a benevolent doctor (played by Forest Whitaker) so that he can have a chance at a 'normal' life. It's a Beauty and the Beast fable which asks, if you feel yourself to be essentially ugly, how can you adapt to life with a handsome face?

Wild Orchid (1990)

From *Johnny Handsome*, it was back to the *9½ Weeks* terrain of erotic melodrama with *Wild Orchid*, directed by softcore impresario (and *9½ Weeks* screenwriter) Zalman King. It's a movie that manages to be strangely compelling without being any good, perhaps because it contains more interesting sexual negotiations than the ludicrous dialogue and *mise en scène* might lead one to believe.[46] *Wild Orchid* is almost exactly modelled on *9½ Weeks*, and like that film, its main characters are a manipulative but highly inarticulate man with a working-class background and an entitled and educated but sexually repressed middle-class woman. Like *9½ Weeks*, it features an episodic plot that introduces the nice middle-class girl (in this case, a lawyer named Emily Reed) to an escalating series of 'dangerous' sexual encounters. The film is set in Rio de Janeiro during carnival, which presents ample opportunities for exoticism. With a colourful set and costumes and a pulsing Latin score, *Wild Orchid* looks and feels even more like a music video than *9½ Weeks* did. Carré Otis, who played Emily Reed, has described the working conditions of the film as unpleasant – and not just because of the poor treatment she received from King and from Rourke (who was her boyfriend and soon-to-be husband at the time, and seemed to be going through an unsavoury period of behaviour): 'our production values appeared to stand in stark contrast to the immense poverty that existed there. It didn't seem to me that we were giving much back to the locals, and the ramifications of that neglect seemed more and more real.'[47] There was flooding in the area during the production, and Otis recalls 'a dark sea of confusion around this film' that 'represented abuse, darkness, exploitation' (Otis's comments are a more stark version of the complaints Kim Basinger had made about her discomfort working with Lyne and Rourke on *9½ Weeks*).[48] No one in the film turned in a strong performance, including Rourke. With fresh plastic surgery, his face was no longer the acting instrument it had once been. And playing the role of Wheeler, a real-estate mogul, Rourke did not seem to have done his usual homework in developing a complex, multi-dimensional character.

As he did in *Diner*, in *Wild Orchid* Rourke once again played a sexual pedagogue and voyeur. He was back in character as a counsellor, pimp and unavailable lover. In this register, perhaps the oddest scene in *Wild Orchid* involves two characters named Otto and

Hannah Munch, a German couple whose relationship has flagged sexually. Rourke's character Wheeler helps them get back on track. He takes the husband Otto out on a Harley Davidson ride to help him fulfil a lost dream. Then, at an outdoor dance party, Hannah is accosted and has her dress ripped, exposing her breasts. In a tinted limo ride back to the hotel, Wheeler orchestrates their reunion, leading to a scene in which they actually have sex in front of him and Emily in the car. It's a bizarre episode, with Rourke's character functioning partly as marriage counsellor to the Munchs and partly as suitor to Emily, courting her by showing off his sexual reconciliation skills. He instils just enough jealousy in the man to make him desire his own wife again. She has been hurt by his sexual neglect, which led (Wheeler guesses) to her infidelity, and is angry at her husband's indifference. 'Don't cover me up. You don't like the way I look? What's wrong with you?' she asks, making a scene and bringing Wheeler in as a witness to her abandonment. And, like a lawyer in the sex-starved wife's defence, Wheeler sets about teaching Otto about a wife's right to sexual fulfilment. Wheeler is on the side of a woman's pleasure, not a man's honour. Just as Hannah has begun to accept that she will never get her husband's attention and starts to pull her clothes back on, Wheeler says, 'Don't. Don't cover up. I want to look at you. That's what you want, isn't it?' He continues to inventory her charms:

You have perfect skin. You have very beautiful breasts. You have a nice hard, flat stomach like swimmers. You haven't had a child, have you? That's right, Otto. Look at your wife. She's beautiful, spirited. What happened to make you so angry? Did you find her with another man? Did you push her into his arms? She liked it? Was that it? Are you punishing her because she liked it?

Otto doesn't respond, so Wheeler ups the ante, actually moving Otto's hands onto his wife's thighs, teaching him how to translate his anger and jealousy into new lust (keep in mind that all of this is

happening in a limo speeding through the Brazilian countryside).
Wheeler proceeds to replay the whole imaginary scene of Hannah's
adultery, somehow healing the couple's wounds. Emily stares
nervously at the German couple as they make love in the moving car.
It's a long and strange scene.

After orchestrating this reunion, Wheeler receives a necklace
as a token of gratitude, and this he offers as a gesture of seduction to
Emily. The next step? He now tries to convince her to move beyond
her bourgeois prejudices about prostitution. When she's horrified
after being propositioned for paid sex by an American tourist, he asks
her why she's so upset:

WHEELER: Is that so bad? To want someone so much that you're willing to
                      pay for it? This is infinitely more exciting.
EMILY: To who?
WHEELER: To you. To me. And if you didn't want to play, Emily, you
                      wouldn't be here.

At this point, Emily realises that there is more at stake in Wheeler's
machinations than merely her carnal education. Her sexually and
emotionally frozen mentor is living vicariously through her. She asks
him: 'You don't touch, so you're touching through me. You don't
feel, so you're feeling through me. Is that it?' Just exactly who is
touching whom, and who is feeling for whom, is unclear. Is Wheeler
gratifying his desire to touch a man through Emily? Or is he
gratifying his desire to touch Emily through another man? We are left
to ponder these questions as Emily goes off with the American john.
We soon see Wheeler lingering below their hotel room, witnessing
through the window the sex scene between them. Here again are
Genet's themes of entangled desire and identification, and the
proliferating possibilities of the threesome. As Wheeler watches them
having sex, Rourke's acting remains cryptic: deep breaths, biting his
lip, eyes roaming up and down. His characters of this period inhabit

a kind of tortured conflict: in *9½ Weeks* it is interiorised (does he desire Elizabeth or want to be her?), while in *Wild Orchid* it is dramatised in threesomes that seem to involve the manipulation of women as a form of repressed sexual desire for men.

Wild Orchid may be the only piece of Hollywood erotica premised so intensely around the trauma of a man's inability to perform. This problem lies at the centre of the plot, as Wheeler concocts a variety of erotic stunts for the women in his life because he cannot claim them sexually. Whether his problem is psychological or physical is never made entirely clear, but it is overcome by the end of the film: *Wild Orchid*'s climax is literally a climax, when Emily finally goads Wheeler into a satisfying bout of lovemaking. The film in some ways recalls the plot of Tennessee Williams's *Cat on a Hot Tin Roof*, the story of lusty Maggie the Cat's quest to win the attention of her handsome but indifferent husband. The final scene gives us Wheeler's own account of the roots of his sexual problem. It's illuminating for the purposes of understanding where Rourke was at this point in his career. In this scene, Wheeler hides away in the corner of the room, ashamed, and tucks his face down into his shoulder as Emily stares confrontationally at him with her arms crossed. He crouches on his haunches between the two lace drapes that now resemble theatre curtains, fondles a rosary and tells her his life story. It's likely that Rourke had a hand in penning this monologue (he frequently contributes his own material to films, such as the final wrestling-ring speech in *The Wrestler*). The *Wild Orchid* monologue bears all the thematic hallmarks of a Rourke-authored scene of the kind he learned to develop at the Actors Studio:

I had a father for a while, and we lived, uh, in a little room. It was by the water.
We talked a lot about not having any money. He taught me how to swim.
When he disappeared, when he disappeared … I barely spoke for years.
I stayed in the third grade for a long time. You know the teachers thought I was
retarded. You know, so they just … they let me put my head down on the desk.

I didn't want to ask any questions, you know, 'cause I was afraid. I worked day and night, and when I was sixteen, I bought my first house, on the worst block in the city, and I fixed it up. Then I bought two more, and I kept it rolling, and I got everything I thought that I ever wanted. And it still wasn't enough.

Then the ladies came. You know, the kind that are attracted to success. It didn't matter to them that I stuttered, that I could barely speak. You know, the more remote that I became, the more they liked it. You know, they took it as a sign of strength. So I started playing games, you know, just to keep it interesting. And uh, the games became a way of life. You know, a maze. I realise now that I couldn't get out of it even if I wanted to.

Here, Rourke adopts the role of a male ice princess. The cause of his coldness is unknown to the women around him, and even his explanatory final monologue about growing up poor and bullied can't fully explain what prevents him from having sexual relationships with women. What Rourke seems to want to express in *Wild Orchid* and *9½ Weeks* – what his monologue reveals, even as it works against the tide of Zalman King's erotica – is the cost of such objectification and forced performance of desire. When Rourke took control of his screen appearances more directly as a writer (in *Homeboy*, *The Last Ride* and *Bullet*), this is what he would dedicate himself to showing. 'The more remote that I became, the more they liked it.' Here, Wheeler reflects on the ethics of the charismatic formula that had been one secret of Rourke's box-office success: how much remoteness and how much intimacy were required from an actor who was performing the function of a sex worker? And what would happen if he ever dropped the mask?

Unfortunately, *Wild Orchid* was too weak and generically inappropriate to vocalise these questions seriously. Rourke's appearance in the film signalled an artist who had stopped surrounding himself with strong colleagues who were his equals. He seems to have been more than usually responsible for his costume decisions, since his character wears the very same clothes and accessories that Rourke was wearing off screen during this period – baggy, oversized suits, sunglasses, bandanas, leather jackets and gold jewellery. Inexplicably, halfway through the film, he simply stops wearing shirts, exposing his waxed, tanned, gym-buffed chest. Rourke had many offers to make the kind of dramatic films in which nobody would have questioned his masculinity or sexuality (*Rain Man*, for example, which went to Tom Cruise). But what he did instead was explore gender and sexual ambiguity on camera by taking on taboo subjects, and in so doing had to pay the same price as many female performers who enter this terrain. The 1970s culture of androgyny and fluidity that had produced the likes of Rourke's youthful idol David Bowie was gone, and in its place the 1980s had brought the macho warrior masculinity of Schwarzenegger and Stallone. In this culture, Rourke had to endure derision and knocks to his credibility as an artist, along with the pressure to continue supplying the same softcore thrills. But all the while, he was getting older.

3 FIGHTER

I'll be real honest. I'm never, ever going to be the caliber of fighter of
James Toney, you know what I'm saying? I know that. I've come to terms
with that. But you know, you take Alec Baldwin and Daniel Day-Lewis and
Kevin Costner, all of them, you put me in a room with those guys, I'll eat
their asshole.

Mickey Rourke, 1994

Having outgrown first the skinny, awkward boyishness of *Body Heat*
and *Diner*, and then the bona fide movie-star handsomeness of
9½ Weeks and *Angel Heart*, Rourke's features filled out and he took
on a puffy, leathery look, which appeared to be the result of cheek
implants and artificial tanning. Rourke's memorable turn in Barbet
Schroeder's *Barfly* and his self-revealing performance in *Johnny
Handsome* marked the end of his career as a contender, and he now
turned away from 'serious' performances towards tough-guy scripts
and softcore spinoffs. His appearances in Simon Wincer's *Harley
Davidson and the Marlboro Man* (1991) and Zalman King's *Wild
Orchid* typify this embarrassing transitional phase. *Wild Orchid* was
roundly panned as a poor attempt to cash in on the success of
9½ Weeks. With *Harley Davidson and the Marlboro Man*, co-starring
Don Johnson, Rourke seemed to be making every effort to demote
himself to the B-list. He explained in later interviews that his
decisions about which films to make at this time were the result of

financial pressures and the impending loss of his house, and that the script choices he made in the late 1980s and early 1990s fuelled self-loathing and a sense of lost direction that precipitated his departure from Hollywood. In his media appearances, Rourke seemed delusional and on the verge of a nervous breakdown. In a 1994 piece on British television (Terry Christian's *The Word* on Channel 4), Rourke's segment began with the announcer calling him 'the man the press have dubbed "Mental Mickey"'. In the accompanying interview, a notably agitated and seemingly manic Rourke, dressed in colourful athletic gear, spewed bile at the film industry and at his own profession:

I don't particularly care for actors. I don't like them ... I just don't like them. I think they're a bunch of people that live in a bubble. You know, I met Warren Beatty one time. I thought, this is one of the creepiest puke-asses I've ever met in my life. I mean, come on. I've got an old friend that's a shoemaker that I've got more respect for.

He also confessed to the interviewer: 'I blew all my money. ... I just lost a three and a half million dollar house, and I've blown, you know, probably twenty million.' As he headed towards forty, Rourke was falling apart, both personally and as an artist. In a 1994 interview on *Late Night with David Letterman* (his first-ever American talk-show appearance), he was noticeably uncomfortable in the face of Letterman's proddings, clutching at his chihuahua as he tried to disappear into his oversized blazer.

Rourke's announcement that he would depart from Hollywood to pursue a career as a professional boxer seems, in retrospect, similar to other highly public disintegrations of talented but troubled stars vexed by the intersection of fame, class and fast living, such as Robert Downey Jr, Lindsay Lohan, Mel Gibson and Charlie Sheen. A boxing career represented a chance to save his soul – and also his masculinity – from an industry that threatened both. But during this period, Rourke didn't disappear as a film artist as completely as it might have seemed. Though no longer a major force in Hollywood during his boxing years, he was actually busy writing and starring in three independent films, *Homeboy* (1988), *FTW, or The Last Ride* (1994) and *Bullet* (1996), each of which, as we might expect, has an athlete for a protagonist (boxer, rodeo rider and baseball player). And even though he was not a particularly good professional fighter, boxing was a crucial influence on Rourke's acting, and it is helpful to recognise that the dynamics of boxing, and especially the art of the counterpunch, flow through his pacing and technique as an actor.

Rourke's appeal as an actor derives from mixed signals, a sense of both hiding and showing. In an interview on the press tour for *The Wrestler*, he explained that boxers, unlike wrestlers, always have to hide their next move: victory depends on surprising an opponent with the angle, strength or timing of a hit. If in the ring Rourke wasn't much to write home about, in front of the camera he was one hell of a boxer. Because he was so good at paying attention, hiding his cards and coming out of nowhere, he could unexpectedly flip the meaning of scenes. His art was one of attunement, obliquity and reflexes. He thrived on redirecting energy, never approaching any line or character straight on. In dramatic conflicts, he never yelled in that tiresome way some actors do. Instead, he withdrew, lay in wait, knew the power of surprise. He could change in a flash. This is his mode in *9½ Weeks*: one minute he's a psychological terrorist, and the next he's playfully convincing his partner, 'You love this game'. He behaves similarly in *Diner* when he threatens to abandon his prankster friend Fenwick (Kevin Bacon) at the side of the road in a flipped car, then suddenly softens and decides to help him out. In group scenes, he wasn't particularly interesting: he shone in these one-on-one matches, especially when he had chemistry with an opponent. Barry Levinson noted the curveball quality, and said of directing him in *Diner*:

There was something about him where you couldn't take your eyes off him. He was this flashy guy, tough, but audiences responded to the sensitivity beneath it all. I think that's the side Mickey would like to hide. And his trying to hide it makes it even more fascinating.[1]

The float-like-a-butterfly/sting-like-a-bee quality of Rourke's acting owed as much to the ring as it did to the Actors Studio.[2]

Rourke had first boxed as a twelve-year-old in Miami, and had suffered a few concussions in those early years. From 1964 to 1972, he participated in twenty-six fights (IMDb claims that he won the first twelve by knockout, though records on Rourke's boxing career are patchy). When he returned to the ring after having achieved success as an actor, he gave a variety of reasons, though an attempt to find a realm of 'reality' distinct from the superficiality of Hollywood was the common note in interviews. He told one reporter that he returned to boxing because he wanted to see if he could 'still do it for real'. We can think of this pursuit of the real in terms of Rourke's anti-theatricality, his quest to narrow the gap between art and life. He took his return to boxing seriously, as seriously as he had his work as an actor. This time his esteemed mentor was the former pro boxer Freddie Roach, and instead of the Actors Studio, Rourke now set up shop with the professionals at Los Angeles's Outlaw Boxing Club. Though treated by the press as something of a slow-moving nervous breakdown, this return to boxing was, for Rourke, a serious pursuit.

Rourke's move into a completely different career, and one with conspicuous materiality, is not unique in the world of Method acting, even beyond the practice of preparing for a role: Daniel Day-Lewis, for instance, once left acting to apprentice himself to a shoemaker in Italy. But Rourke's detour was much more visible. Some of his bouts were recorded (and will live for ever on YouTube). And the director Brett Ratner (a friend of Rourke's, and then at the beginning of his career) followed him to Miami, filmed his training sessions and recorded Rourke's remarks about his turn to boxing as a kind of physical and

spiritual purification.[3] Rourke's ambition was to fight sixteen bouts,
though he stopped after just eight, and the result is well known: he
sustained gruesome injuries to his face, which required several
operations. This new face, which has become a featured exhibit in the
case against plastic surgery, is the inescapable memoir of these years.

Rather than simply a personal crisis, Rourke's high-profile
career flame-out in the early 1990s might be thought of as the result
of an interesting attempt to fuse two traditions (or perhaps to expose
the extent to which they were already fused): Method acting and
pornography (traditions that consciously 'used' the actor, and related
to the audience in a particular way). These traditions were not
necessarily incompatible. The Method had long been tangled up

with issues of male sexuality. As Marlon Brando and Paul Newman's performances in works by Tennessee Williams indicated, homosexuality, sexual secrets and the objectification of men were an important part of the dramatic canon that existed in symbiotic relationship with the Method's development. Rourke pushed these themes to new and uncomfortable levels of visibility. In his three independent films, his primary subject matter was no longer the violation of women by men, but the less broachable topic of the sexual abuse of men, the paralysing effects of class and commodification, and the quest for the transcendence of traumatic memory through extreme moments of physicality, exhibitionism, and athletic and sexual performance. His previous Hollywood performances had given glimpses of these themes. 'I can't get excited,' the supposed lothario John confesses to Elizabeth in *9½ Weeks* as he pushes her to further extremes of experience. 'What does it feel like to be out of control?' he calls out after her as he chases her from a room in the Chelsea Hotel through the crowded streets of the city. However bizarre Rourke's role choices in the late 1980s seemed, they were united by this sense of crisis, and by a painful inability to connect to sensation first hand.

At the lowest point of his acting career, when he was making films like *Harley Davidson and the Marlboro Man*, the general consensus was that this 'fine young actor' was recreating himself as a 'stumbling hack, without range, without craft, without even giving a damn'.[4] But Rourke's three independent films from this period (which he also wrote) – *Homeboy*, *FTW, or The Last Ride* and *Bullet* – show him beginning to search for a visual language to communicate the constellation of themes that obsessed him.[5] Removing dialogue, relying increasingly on gesture and music, in these performances Rourke excessively foregrounded his objectification in an effort to exceed it, to come out finally on the other side of fetish and cliché. These three films are the work of an actor who was fading away from stardom and losing his hold on the public, but they are not worthless.

Though they made no critical or commercial impact, we can see what Rourke was trying to do, and what, with Darren Aronofsky's help, he was finally able to achieve in a critically legible way in *The Wrestler*: to use the tools of both melodrama and tragedy to depict an abused and self-destructive athlete with compassion. Perhaps we should think of these films as dress rehearsals for his breathtaking performance in *The Wrestler*.

Rourke's athlete protagonists have greater articulacy of body than of speech, a quality that has sometimes led critics to identify the actor himself as an unreflective lout. 'To inhabit characters of dubious artistic value', wrote Cintra Wilson of Rourke's success, it is helpful if actors 'aren't terribly smart'.[6] But here Wilson plays into the hands of Rourke's primitivist style. Rourke's apparent 'dumbness' inhabits a negative stereotype about athletes, and works as a defensive posture. It is also a marker of trauma, of what cannot be communicated in words. But on screen, through some cinematic alchemy, his 'dumbness' becomes heartbreaking and expressive, a poetics of the dumb. In some of his best performances, we can see Rourke playing dumb in three related ways. First, he expresses the experience of 'dumb guys', the under-educated, misinformed or slow on the draw. Second, his characters are literally dumb, sometimes to the point of muteness. Third, as the energies of speech are drawn inward and dispersed throughout the body, Rourke becomes an actor of gesture who transmits emotion kinaesthetically.

Even before developing his athlete protagonists, Rourke had a long history of playing 'dumb guys', usually dreamers who have a hard time making their dreams come true. Though they often have some compensating quality – charm, wisdom, kindness, toughness – Rourke exposes how, inevitably, the lack of cleverness takes its toll. Boogie in *Diner* can't hack it in law school and ends up in construction; Motorcycle Boy in *Rumble Fish* seems to have some kind of cosmic knowledge, but no way of articulating it; Charlie Moran in *The Pope of Greenwich Village* just can't figure out how to get his own restaurant. Rourke's silent men bear all the marks of the survivor of childhood abuse: rage, fear, helplessness, isolation, alienation and perpetual feelings of loss, shame and guilt, as well as a seemingly irresistible drive to destroy close relationships. In *Johnny Handsome*, Rourke plays a criminal whose mouth is so misshapen that his words are incomprehensible. But even when a surgical intervention gives him a chance at speech and a rehabilitated life, he can't make himself heard. The silence is more than skin-deep, and he slides back into a life of crime that eventually kills him. Rourke's virtuosic ability to perform inarticulacy reached new heights in the figure of the brain-damaged boxer Johnny Walker in *Homeboy*, who doesn't even know the word for an apple. And this performance of voicelessness intensifies in each of Rourke's three self-authored films. In each, he plays a character who seems at first more like a patchwork of fetishes than a human being, as he hyperbolically inhabits pornographic fantasies: cowboy boots, cigarettes, boxing gloves, denim and tattoos. Rourke plays wrongfully convicted felons in two cases: an ex-con rodeo rider in *FTW, or The Last Ride*, and an ex-con Jewish gangster in *Bullet*. Employing a strategy that anticipates *The Wrestler*, in these films Rourke inhabits the abject, commodified man, the most clichéd exterior, with immensely individualised, verisimilistic performances, so that his characters are both fetish and human at the same time. In this way, he brings together the reifying aesthetic of pornography with the personalising, intensely emotional effects of Method acting. Rourke signals from within, not flattening his characters into objects of sex or violence, but dramatising the psychic effects of such objectification. He plays types whom others see as clichés, but who don't know that they're clichés, and whose suffering is no less real for that reason. Rourke plays these roles as if in an iron mask, his eyes and posture transmitting the messages that his words cannot. Later, in *The Wrestler*, which continues the pattern, we meet a Rourke who is not just dumb, but also going blind and deaf, with bifocals and hearing aid on display.

Homeboy was shot in Bruce Springsteen's hometown of Asbury Park, New Jersey, and its boxing scenes were filmed in the boardwalk's Convention Hall (where scenes for *The Wrestler* would be shot twenty years later). *Homeboy* is loosely based on the story of a down-and-out boxer Rourke had known in his youth. The film traces the alcoholic Johnny from his arrival in town on a rainy night, through his attempt to revive his boxing career, his brief but sweet romance with a carnival worker named Ruby whom he meets on the boardwalk (played by Rourke's first wife Debra Feuer) and his ultimate fatal knockout in the boxing ring. It bears the generic hallmarks of the boxing film, but does not glorify any of its aspects: there is no hope of a real comeback. One of Johnny Walker's final speeches echoes, in the interrogative, Brando's 'could've been a contender' speech from *On the Waterfront* (1954), with its lament for wasted opportunity: acknowledging the squandering of his own talent, Walker asks, 'you think I coulda been good?' The dramatic stakes of the plot are heightened by the information (delivered partway through the film) that Walker is suffering from a skull fracture and that the next harsh blow might kill him. His corrupt manager (played by Rourke's old Actors Studio friend Christopher Walken) chooses not to tell him about this injury. The melancholy score by Eric Clapton emphasises the down-and-out blues themes of the plot and prevents *Homeboy* from ever setting foot on the feel-good terrain of *Rocky*. Filmed during weekends while Rourke was working on *9½ Weeks* in New York, *Homeboy* reveals a different side of the sleek 1980s playboy.

Homeboy's excruciatingly lonely protagonist simply cannot muster the words necessary to get help or make the human connections he so desperately craves. Exploited by managers and hangers-on, Johnny can only express himself through the violence of the boxing ring, a violence that becomes ecstatic in the film's final scene. This gap between the desire to make himself understood and the inability to marshal language is registered in his agonisingly trite,

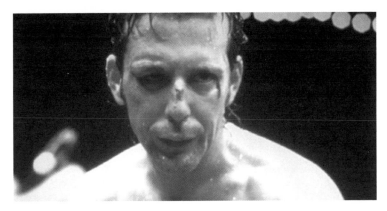

Rourke in the first of three movies he wrote,
Homeboy (1988)

halting speech about his passion for Ruby. Monosyllabic, trailing off
in incomplete thoughts, Johnny's monologue contrasts sharply with
the smooth way other men in the film talk about women:

That Ruby, she's a good one. She's so pretty. Man I'd just like to be able to look
at her and just ... I could just look at her and just hold her and ... I'd like her to
just touch me, just, you know, just touch me and have her like me, you know.

Holding his jaw as though it's been broken too many times and is
now permanently wired shut, Rourke dramatises the problem of
speaking *for* the Johnny Walkers of the world.

This silence becomes more than an expression of blank
suffering and unspeakable violation in Rourke's performances,
thanks to his physical articulacy, his gift for expression through
movement. 'He could break your heart with a look,' wrote Bob
Dylan of Rourke's performance in *Homeboy*: 'The movie traveled
to the moon every time he came onto the screen. Nobody could
hold a candle to him. He was just there, didn't have to say hello or
goodbye.'[7] Dylan's sense of Rourke's quiet presence picks up on his

use in *Homeboy* of an archive of Chaplinesque moments of pathos, from Johnny's hitching up of the collar of his denim jacket to deflect the rain, to his pathetic sharing of a sandwich with Ruby, to his careful recovery of a single coin from his bureau. Here we see Rourke inhabiting the long theatrical and cinematic lineage of melodrama, with its tendency to elaborate plot through movement set to music. The film is also indebted to the melodramatic tradition in its division into stock characters: a well-meaning but hapless protagonist (Rourke), a scheming villain (Walken) and a heroine in need of rescuing (Feuer), as well as in its highly emotional tenor, its threat of the protagonist's untimely death and its sense that Rourke and Feuer's characters, the lovers, are hemmed in on all sides by a cruel and unfeeling world, with only each other to rely upon.

Each Rourke-helmed film increasingly reveals the unspoken fact at the heart of his character's silence: rape. In *Homeboy*, the possibility of sexual violation is raised only in the significant silence following Johnny's confession of the childhood that shaped him. Rourke uses an Actors Studio-inspired emotion memory exercise not only as a technique for connecting to the emotional truth of a scene, but also as the template for the dramatic scene itself. Johnny finds that a coin-fed mechanical horse triggers a memory of his loss of childhood security:

Oh God Damn. Hey I ain't seen one of these in a long time. Well, I remember when I was a boy I used to always ask my granny for a nickel so I could ride on one of these. ... Can I sit on it? ... I used to ask her for some nickels, and she'd give me a whole bunch of nickels to ride on the horses, and get me candy. I really liked that. I spent a lot of time with my old granny, 'cause my mother, she was fucking nuts. And my old man, he just drank himself to death. And then my old granny died. They sent me to this place where there was all these boys like me. I didn't like them, man, I didn't like none of them. I used to try to run back home, I just didn't know how to get there.

Whatever happened to Johnny at this place is left unsaid, but Rourke's delivery of these lines reveals the pain and confusion beneath the biographical mumbling.

The currents of sexual abuse become more explicit in his next film, *FTW, or The Last Ride*, in which Rourke's character, Frank T. Wells, meets a vigilante named Scarlett who slowly reveals that she was raped by her brother. As their biographies merge, Frank overcomes the impotence instilled by prison through hearing her story. *FTW* is a classic Western in its landscapes and cinematography, but probes deeper than the average Western into the spiritual kinship between abused men and women, showing them as fellow outlaws in a manner that revises the dynamic of the recently released feminist classic *Thelma and Louise* (1991) and which, in its investigation of the repressed sexual dynamics of the American West, also anticipates *Brokeback Mountain* (2005). *FTW* displaces the working out of male sexual violation onto the body of a woman, but Rourke's next film addresses the legacies of a raped man directly.

In *Bullet*, a meandering and atmospheric heist picture set in Brooklyn, the film's imagery goes furthest in suggesting the source of shame. Rourke plays the title character, whose first act upon being released from prison is the attempted rape of two young men during a hold-up. When he gets home to his family, he tries to tell his father what happened to him in prison, and then he tries again while in a hotel bedroom with an exotic dancer, confessing his impotence with honesty and self-loathing: 'it's no good, it's dead'. When the dancer departs, the failed phallus is replaced by the penetration of a drug needle and Bullet passes out in a combined nightmare/fantasy montage of eroticised men's bodies recalled from prison. Bullet tries to bring up his sexual confusion with his best friend, explaining his theory that his friend is a 'repressed homosexual'. 'You don't have to suck dick to be a queer,' he tells him. 'You gonna tell me you never looked at another guy and thought about it?', a question constructed in a way that allows his friend to respond ambiguously: 'No. Nah.'

Bullet belongs firmly to the age of Tarantino, with its tough-talking criminals and frenetic urban visual style. Directed by Rourke's friend Julien Temple, *Bullet* is a brutal extension of the themes of *Homeboy*. Butch 'Bullet' Stein, a Jewish drug user and petty criminal from Brooklyn, returns to his old life after spending eight years in jail. But this is no redemption tale. Bullet quickly falls back into drug use and theft. He soon enough clashes with a local drug dealer named Tank (played by Tupac Shakur), who subsequently kills Bullet at the film's end. *Bullet* is a tragedy, as Rourke and Shakur's characters are both ground out by a cyclical violence that has no discernible beginning or end (and in a particularly brutal case of life reflecting art, Shakur was murdered soon after the film was completed). Although *Bullet* belongs to Rourke's 'lost' period, made up of little-watched films and much-hyped boxing matches, it is not a complete failure. Wearing a tracksuit and wool hat pulled down low over his eyes, Rourke, as ever, is fascinating on screen, particularly in his ability to hold the viewer's attention with almost no dialogue. And Adrien Brody turns in a strong early performance as Bullet's younger brother, a mural artist from Coney Island, whose creative presence is counterpointed against the film's drive towards annihilation. Taken within the arc of Rourke's career, *Bullet* is itself a version of Brody's character, a slight glimmer of light amidst a time of confusion and transition.

As Rourke was making his own low-profile films, his acting gift had not been entirely forgotten in Hollywood. Nearly twenty years after they had worked together on *Rumble Fish*, Francis Ford Coppola cast Rourke in his adaptation of John Grisham's *The Rainmaker* (1997), as the womanising, ambulance-chasing lawyer Bruiser Stone. In 2000, Steve Buscemi asked Rourke to play a transgender prison inmate opposite Edward Furlong in *Animal Factory*. And in 2001, he turned in a melodramatic cameo in Sean Penn's *The Pledge* as a father whose daughter has been kidnapped, playing a compelling scene opposite Jack Nicholson. Then came

Rourke's breakthrough comeback performance in Robert Rodriguez and Frank Miller's *Sin City* (2005). By the time Darren Aronofsky came knocking on his door, Rourke was an actor in his fifties, humbled by experience and haunted by failure, more than two decades away from the cocky heights of *9½ Weeks*, and as hungry for recognition and respect as he'd been when he first arrived in New York in the 1970s. He was about to embark on one of the most dramatic second acts in recent Hollywood history.

Comeback

In wrestling, a man who is down is exaggeratedly so, and completely fills the eyes of the spectators with the intolerable spectacle of his powerlessness.

Roland Barthes, 'The World of Wrestling'[8]

No one believed in Mickey Rourke ... He has no value as a commodity. Well, I sat across from him and looked into his eyes. His eyes aren't dead. They're alive, yearning, thinking.

Darren Aronofsky[9]

At the 2009 Academy Awards, Mickey Rourke, front-runner and favourite, lost the Best Actor prize to his old friend and rival Sean Penn. Though Rourke's performance in *The Wrestler* had been universally acclaimed, it was Penn's turn as San Francisco city councilman Harvey Milk that took the Oscar. Rourke had played the anti-hero Randy the Ram, a trashy, washed-up and politically incorrect professional wrestler, socially defunct, a man disconnected from the larger social and political struggles of his time, however much he may have been a symptom of them. In Gus Van Sant's *Milk* (2008), Penn played America's first openly gay elected official in a year in which the Proposition 8 trials had made Milk's folk-hero status newly relevant, and had made the civil rights he championed earlier (against Proposition 6, which would have mandated the firing of gay teachers) the most pressing cause in California. The win – Penn's second in the category, and his fifth nomination – confirmed his status as the industry's favourite bad boy. Rourke, meanwhile, had never been nominated before, and it seemed only right that this weathered figure who had always thrown in his lot with life's losers would walk away empty-handed. Though Rourke's performance in *The Wrestler* had generated critical adulation, media attention, and a string of independent and European awards, he was still not granted Hollywood's highest honour. Compounding the sense of Rourke's bad luck, two years later Natalie Portman would take home an Academy Award for the 'hers' version of Rourke's performance in *The Wrestler* when she played a masochistic ballerina in Aronofsky's *Black Swan* (2010).

The Wrestler was Aronofsky's fourth feature film, and its low-key handheld camera style represented a change from his more experimental, self-conscious early films. Reviewers were almost unanimous in their praise, lauding *The Wrestler* for its simplicity and earnestness, as well as for the way that Rourke's performance breathed pathos and depth into what might have been a formulaic sports comeback film. 'A straightforward tale, given tremendous extra punch by its leading man,' was Anthony Lane's verdict, who also noted Rourke's masochism: 'No one else, it seems fair to say, could have played the part; for one thing, no one but Rourke combines a gently spoken sweetness with so glazed and inflated a physique, together with a willingness to be treated by his peers like a veal chop.'[10] Amy Biacolli wrote in the *Houston Chronicle* that 'this sad, strong beast of a film keeps us pinned to the mat with the strength of its compassion and the overpowering force of its central performance. And what a shocker it is. What a gutsy and vulnerable piece of work from one of American cinema's most battle-worn, and fascinating, stars.'[11] Noting the performance's roots in Method acting, Rourke's hometown paper, the *Miami Herald*, wrote '*The*

Wrestler is one of those pictures where the lines between performer and character are intentionally blurred for dramatic gain.'[12] London's *Time Out* praised Aronofsky for clearing a space for his actor-auteur: 'His biggest contribution is to stand aside and let Rourke go to work.'[13] Also noting, as many critics did, the biographical parallels to Rourke's own life, *Time Out* suggests that 'while the role is loaded, Rourke never coasts, delivering a committed, sympathetic portrait of a humble man cornered by bad decisions'. Peter Bradshaw called Rourke 'sublimely cast'.[14] 'This is the performance of his lifetime', wrote Roger Ebert, delivering the long view. He continued, 'I cared as deeply about Randy the Ram as any movie character I've seen this year. I cared about Mickey Rourke, too. The way this role and this film unfold, that almost amounts to the same thing.'[15] Kenneth Turan of the *LA Times* didn't like the film, but still loved Rourke, citing 'a lead performance that is everything it could possibly be'.[16]

Were it not for the vulnerability, contradiction and regret that Rourke revealed in his portrayal of Randy Robinson, audiences might understandably have been put off by *The Wrestler*'s violence and also by the aggressive white working-class masculinity that it seemed, if not to glorify, then at least to mourn for. The 2009 Academy Awards followed one month after the inauguration of Barack Obama, a moment that signalled a transition from the kind of vigilante leadership shown by George W. Bush to the deliberative common sense and carefulness of Obama. Randy the Ram, an icon of battered and besieged white warrior masculinity, is depicted sympathetically in Aronofsky's film as a tragic victim of capitalism and the sports industry. Hence, this could easily be interpreted as a reactionary film that pities the plumage, but forgets the dying bird: a film that elicits sympathy for the decline of one white warrior in the style of Schwarzenegger and Bush. Indeed, Rourke, himself mistaking an overlord for an underdog, spoke up in defence of Bush at a time when few others were willing to defend him, telling *GQ* magazine that 'President Bush was in the wrong place at the wrong time, I don't know how anyone could have handled this situation,' and that it is 'too easy to blame everything on one guy. These are unpredictable, dangerous times, and I don't think that anyone really knows quite what to do.'[17] Off screen, Rourke seemed determined to stand for everything beyond the pale of liberal discourse. On a drunken night out, he brushed off unwanted paparazzi by calling them 'faggots', then defended his right to the slur, saying 'Look, I'm not afraid to say the word "fag" ... I've got plenty of gay friends. We toss the word around.'[18] (After sobering up, he delivered the requisite apology via his publicist.) Though he was not active in any political party, Rourke's comments seemed to align him with the Wild West-style Republicanism of John Wayne, Arnold Schwarzenegger, Clint Eastwood and Jon Voight. But always drawn to the plight of common people, he also appeared alongside old lefty Kris Kristofferson in the video for John Rich's 'Shuttin' Detroit Down' in 2009: while Kristofferson plays a plant worker who loses his job after years of service, Rourke plays the friend who gets angry on his behalf. In 2009, Rourke toured the media circuit as a sentimental old-school man, unchastened by identity politics or political correctness. When awarded a pair of 'Mantlers' at Spike TV's Guy's Choice Awards, Rourke pulled a serviceman from the audience and handed the award over to him with the words:

There are a whole bunch of soldier boys – men – here, and I just want to give a shout-out to everybody. So I was thinking, earlier on, 'What the fuck am I gonna do with those antlers in my house? I would rather they be on the front of some tank in Afghanistan or Iraq where they're kicking ass! So I'd like Calderon to come up here and bring this back to wherever you guys are kicking ass. I wanna give this to you. Soldier Calderon ... get your ass up here motherfucker!

They hug, and then Calderon proclaims, 'This goes out to all the soldiers that have fallen, and everybody still fighting around the world. Thank you very much! Thank you!' Clearly, in the wake of *The Wrestler*, Rourke filled his fans' emotional need for some old-school male bonding.

In *The Wrestler*, however, such male bonding has a more fleeting quality. Rourke delivers an extravagant performance of working-class male victimisation, playing a character whose life is divorced from any notion of political solidarity. The only forms of community that can provide temporary comfort come from the fellowship of other wrestlers and wrestling audiences, a fellowship of blood and mutual isolation. It is an extraordinarily unempowering film, a film that conspicuously refuses every opportunity to make points about domestic political issues such as health care (Randy is broke, but his visit to the hospital is somehow mysteriously paid for). And yet perhaps the film's very insistence on eliding the larger political and social structures that determine his life and the lives of others around him captures the experience of adriftness and mystification that keep people like Randy in their current station. It is helpful to view the dynamics of Aronofsky's film, and Rourke's performance in it, in terms of David Savran's model of 'self-reflexive sadomasochism'. In *Taking It Like a Man*,[19] Savran argues that the mode of white male self-fashioning since the 1970s, and particularly in response to the rise of identity politics, has been reactionary. Denied cultural hegemony, American white men have developed a masochistic style of backlash that is fed by a feeling of powerlessness, a dynamic that can be identified across a broad cultural swathe from Southern Rock to *Rambo*. In other words, because they can no longer lash out at others, they flagellate themselves.

But the tragedy of Rourke's performance in the film diverged from his new star image. Rourke the star (and person) seemed to have found a kind of happiness at last, and in the wake of his comeback in *The Wrestler*, he emerged not as a tragic victim but as a comic survivor. He also had a different appeal from the one he enjoyed the first time around. Though he had always been popular with male audiences, it was still mostly women who had swooned for him in the 1980s, but now it was men as well. Through the character of Randy the Ram, Rourke gave voice to a widespread feeling of vestigial masculinity, a sense of a male identity that knew itself to be defunct, but couldn't help mourning for itself all the same. Just as Rourke the actor tapped into the tragic theatricality of figures like Oedipus and Lear to become the icon of battered, besieged and superannuated masculinity, Rourke the star became the icon of an ironical, camp, post-feminist machismo, knowing, humorous, *almost* domesticated and declawed. In recognition of his achievement in masculine self-fashioning, this actor who called everyone 'Brother' was awarded *GQ*'s Man of the Year award, along with a series of other pop cultural accolades. Having lost his looks on the altar of experience, and having reframed masochism from sexuality to sport, Rourke returned to fully fledged Hollywood stardom as an endearing elder statesman.

Promoting *The Wrestler*, Rourke and Aronofsky made a compelling duo on the media circuit. Rourke loved to tell the story of his degradation at the hands of this demanding young director. 'You have to do everything I say', Aronofsky had insisted during their first meeting to discuss *The Wrestler*. As Rourke tells the story:

He sort of walked across the street like his balls were too big for his pants ... Then he just started saying, 'You've ruined your career for the last 15 years and I can't raise a dime on your name. If I do this movie with you, you're gonna listen to everything I tell you, you're gonna do everything I say and you can never disrespect me in front of the crew. Oh, and I can't pay you.' I thought, 'This is the kinda guy I want to work with.'[20]

Ever the masochist, in these anecdotes Rourke left no doubt that he was the bottom, there to be beaten up, stapled, gigged and sent to the hospital between takes. The dynamic was captured in Annie Leibowitz's portrait of the sadistic director and his battered muse:

'The Ringers': Darren Aronofsky
and Mickey Rourke, by Annie
Leibowitz (2009)

Aronofsky bursting from his cheap-looking suit, his close-cropped
hair and moustache that screamed masculinity crisis, his
confrontation with the camera; and Rourke crouching in the
background, half-naked, long-haired, smoking, bruised and tattooed,
as though there were nothing you could do to him anymore.
He looked like a boxer in his corner – a pornographic, existential
boxer wearing tight jeans and velvet shoes. The photograph appeared
in the wake of Leibowitz's bare-backed portrait of the fifteen-year-
old Miley Cyrus, and satirists joked that she had taken advantage of
Rourke too, and that there would be

much hand-wringing and fiery debate ... concerning the 'appropriate' way to
depict a 56-year-old former it-boy turned professional boxer turned down-
and-out has-been turned comeback kid, followed by an official statement from

Rourke himself explaining how he 'was so honored and thrilled to work with Annie … and now, seeing the photographs … I feel so embarrassed.'[21]

Leibowitz's image put its finger on the paradox that was Rourke: that this supposed 'man's man' could still project an aura of exploitability which, like Cyrus's, needed a father to protect it. Rourke said of Aronofsky: 'When I met him, I knew this was a guy who would fight for me,' and when he won the Independent Spirit Award, he stood up, grabbed the face of his tormenter and kissed him right on the lips. Rourke dressed like a leatherman, with keys dangling off his belt, and even his chihuahua Loki was named after a Norse god of bondage.

Rourke's persona on late-night talk shows and in awards speeches was that of an ageing rock dandy, full of profanity and bonhomie. He carried his beloved Loki with him everywhere, and when Loki died just before the Academy Awards, Rourke showed up wearing a necklace with the dog's portrait. He often broke down in tears when explaining the loss. Rourke's particular combination of hardness and softness, of masculinity and femininity, was a fascinating spectacle. It harked back to the many gender-ambiguous moments of his earlier film career, particularly the scene in *Diner* in which Boogie offered his penis to his date in a box of popcorn. 'Wanna bet me Carol Heathrow goes for my pecker on the first date?' This defining moment of Rourke's early career was characteristically ambiguous. On the one hand: Touch my pecker! On the other: Take my pecker, please! Was Rourke's character advertising his manhood or his castration envy? 'Soft beneath the manly chest and hard beneath the zipper' was Scott Raab's description of Rourke's appeal as an actor, but his films always call such potency into question.[22]

In *The Wrestler*, it's not clear whether Randy is a 'prick' or a 'pussy'. Both terms circulate throughout the film, turning up in the language of Randy and others. A prick is a contemptible man – usually one with some worldly authority – who has let that power get the better of him. He's imperious, self-aggrandising, selfish, irresponsible. *The Wrestler* leaves us to arbiter between two versions of Randy. Is he the prickish deadbeat dad who ruins the chance to reconcile with his daughter so he can get high and have sex with a stranger, or is he the sweetheart who gives her a touching set of second-hand clothes? This question is never settled. Though Randy is a 'nice guy', he's also a prick. But as always, Rourke inhabits the slur. A prick doesn't experience himself as a prick, he experiences the fact that it's hard out there for a prick. And because of Rourke's disturbingly luminous ability to suffer on screen, the audience experiences that too. But, sap though he is, Randy rejects other emotional men, especially in his musical preference for metal. 'The 80s – best shit ever,' he says. 'Then that Cobain pussy had to come along and ruin it all.' Randy the Ram has given himself a name that's synonymous with aggression, lechery and penetration. His signature move, the 'Ram Jam', involves thrusting his stiffened body into his opponent. But though his character's name parodies macho sexual aggression, the 'off-kilter' quality Pauline Kael sensed in *Diner* is still on display in the tensions between the Herculean beast Randy aspires to be, the frail, isolated man he is and a third, even subtler figure – the Randy who walks up to a pharmacy counter with *Town & Country* magazine in his shopping basket. Randy's aspirations to phallic power are more often sad than threatening. His boss at the grocery store taunts him for wearing tights and 'sitting on other guys' faces'. The protagonist of *The Wrestler* is a man who lives on the margins of the heterosexual family. He sleeps not just in a trailer park, but in a van parked inside a trailer park. Randy lingers by deserted phone booths, under train tracks and near sewers, as though choosing to be received as a prick rather than suspected as a pussy.

In his acting in *The Wrestler*, Rourke uses a layering technique, veering between strength and vulnerability, and masculinity and femininity. Aronofsky goes to great lengths to demonstrate how the wrestler achieves his appearance through steroids, weightlifting,

Blonde bombshell: Rourke in Aronofsky's
The Wrestler (2008)

tanning and hair dye. Rourke's Randy grooms like a woman.
Keeping up his look for the ring means that he lives in a world of
tanning beds and salons (he talks shop with his hairdresser, coaching
her on how long to leave the foils in). His platinum-blonde mane,
his distinctive feature, is often pulled up in a granny-like bun.
These vulnerable touches throw into poignant relief his bulging
wrestler's muscles, weathered face, grungy jeans and plaid shirts.
Here we see the sad young man (Dean, Clift) transformed into the
sad old man (Oedipus, Lear). What is faintly suggested as the source
of his melancholy and of his social estrangement is a transgender
identity that Aronofsky embeds in the film's imagery when Randy
pulls a towel from its rail in the bathroom to reveal the torso of a
naked woman beneath, the secret at the heart of Randy's masculinity?

The suspense of *The Wrestler* revolves around Randy's wavering
gender identity. We are led through a series of incidents in which
Randy is forced to reflect on whether he will be able to accept
domesticity and heterosexuality as the price of human connection.
We also see him wavering between moments of denial and self-harm,
and of awareness and authenticity. Ironically, Randy's prickishness
stems from a failure of patriarchy rather than an excess of it.
When he visits the home of his daughter to make peace, he finds he's

Randy emerging from the shower; two torsos

been replaced by the lesbian phallus in the person of Stephanie's girlfriend. Though Randy ultimately can't get out of the cycle of prickishness, and though Aronofsky makes it clear that a critical understanding of the system he inhabits is beyond his power, the most memorable and moving moments of the film are those in which Randy almost achieves self-awareness, moments of quiet authenticity, fleeting but profound reckonings. In these instances, Randy inhabits not a grandiose pose of martyrdom (which he's a bit too good at), but moments of simple clarity. His character is established early on: dumb, emotionally and physically exhausted, self-centred and with a short fuse. We know, in the words of the Springsteen theme, that no matter how hard Randy tries, he'll always 'leave with less than he had before'. But for all of Randy's incomprehension of the world and his place in it, the drama still turns on these moments of subtle recognition that briefly seduce us into thinking that the fatal ending might be averted.

As is often the case, Rourke's most expressive moments are wordless. First, Randy sits on a mattress in the back of his Dodge Ram post-match. He's been locked out of his trailer for failing to come up with the rent. He opens a can of beer and gazes at the posters and clippings of himself that paper the back doors of his van. He nods his head slightly. What has he just seen? His mortality? His selfishness? We don't know, but we know he's acknowledged some important truth. Randy has another such moment while signing autographs at a fan event. He looks beneath the table at the legs and feet of his fellow wrestlers: wheelchairs, splints. He knows what awaits him. These flickering moments of acknowledgment, presence, accountability pave the way for the big one, Randy's confrontation with his daughter Stephanie. For this scene, the quiet showpiece of *The Wrestler*, Aronofsky films the abandoned New Jersey boardwalk as though it were a backdrop for Greek tragedy – a desolate stage, dotted with occasional ruins – for it is Greek tragedy, a Sophoclean family reckoning. After years in the prickish wilderness, the deadbeat dad takes responsibility – sort of:

I just want to tell you. I'm the one who was supposed to take care of everything. I'm the one who was supposed to make everything OK for everybody. But it just didn't work out like that. And I left. I left you. You never did anything wrong, you know. I used to try to forget about you, I used to try to pretend that you didn't exist. But I can't. You're my girl. And now, I'm an old broken down piece of meat. And I'm alone. And I deserve to be all alone. I just don't want you to hate me. Kay?

So compelling is Rourke's acting in this scene that we don't at first notice Randy's narcissism, the prevalence of the word 'I', the lame excuse that 'it just didn't work out'. As he did as Boogie, here again Rourke plays against unflattering lines, inhabiting them with such longing, honesty and desperation that they begin to mean more than a string of excuses. This moment of intense connection is all the more valuable, all the more regrettable, for its unsustainability. It is the classic Rourke slide from the woman, only this time the stakes are higher – the woman is his daughter.

Rourke's character moves away emotionally even as his physical presence on screen intensifies throughout the film. *The Wrestler* is set in three meat markets: the ring, the strip club and the deli counter where Randy works. The most gruesome scene, and the one that drives home the theme of Randy's flesh as meat, takes place in this last location, as Randy nearly comes to terms with his new, mundane job. Though he faces his shift with dread, as he starts to serve up cold cuts he begins to enjoy himself, and to charm his customers. But suddenly, in a horrifying recognition scene, someone in the deli line outs him as the professional wrestler Randy the Ram. Shamed and enraged by the collision of worlds, by the reminder of his fall from celebrity, Randy lashes out, violently mutilating himself on a meat slicer in front of the staff and customers. Like Boogie's pecker-in-a-box moment in *Diner*, the climax of this film is an ambiguous castration allegory. We see Randy's thumb approach the meat grinder and smash against the running blade. The gesture's meaning goes in two directions: symbolically, we see the destruction of the phallus, the ego, the flesh as signed by the thumb, but narratively we see the return of the phallus, because this is the *peripeteia* (and *The Wrestler* is nothing if not Aristotelian drama), the moment when Randy rejects his emasculating job and decides that he would rather die on his feet in the ring than live on his knees in the supermarket. He storms out of the store, primally smearing blood on his face. When his boss reminds him that there are customers witnessing this horrific display of self-butchery, he retorts, 'You little prick, you gonna talk to me the way you do?' This moment of reversal is structured sadomasochistically.

Grist to the mill of tragedy

Just when Randy has lulled the audience into believing in his submission behind the deli counter, he reasserts control by acting out in a way that tosses the plot in the opposite direction. His act is masochistic, but it turns sadistic as he storms through the store, spraying blood across the cereal aisle.

The meat slicer incident makes it clear that though Randy knows he has failed as a parent and a person, he will live out the phallic lie anyway. Against doctor's orders, he calls his manager and commits to a rematch with his old opponent. In the last wrestling scene, before he makes his ambiguous final leap (either to glory or cardiac arrest), we see Randy straining to get his body erect one more time as he prepares for the film's final Ram Jam. It's easier for Randy to kill himself than to stop being a prick. But this assertion is self-sacrifice too, and the monologue that Rourke developed for his character is an offering up of himself to the wrestling/cinema audience in a moment that blurs the story of Randy the Ram with the story of Mickey Rourke:

A lot of people told me that I'd never wrestle again, and that's all I do. You know if you live hard and you play hard and you burn the candle at both ends, you pay the price for it. You know in this life you can lose everything that you love, everything that loves you. Now I don't hear as good as I used

Randy's final 'Ram Jam'

to, and I forget stuff, and I ain't as pretty as I used to be. But god damn, I'm still standing here, and I'm the Ram. As time goes by … as time goes by they say, 'He's washed up, he's finished, he's a loser, he's all through', but you know what? The only ones who are gonna tell me when I'm through doing my thing is you people here. You people here. You people here are the ones worth bringing it for because you're my family. I love all of you. Thank you so much.

It is the first of the film's wrestling scenes to be shot in a theatre rather than a gym, a setting that drives home the point that the comeback is Rourke's as well as Randy's. Bursting into the ring with heavy-metal hair, wristbands and green sequin spandex tights, Rourke hits many major themes of his career: the rock 'n' roll theatricality, the embrace of victimisation, the celebration of excess, the willingness to 'pay the price', the attempt to create an alternative family and the offering of pleasure to others through the endurance of pain. Now that Randy/Rourke is stripped of all his resources – face, money, stardom, youth – it's clear that these weren't the sources of his attraction after all. All along he was giving pleasure with his mixed signals, his ways of paying attention, of revealing and hiding, of offering himself up for a beating, of expressing pain. By going backstage at the wrestling match, by showing the staples being removed from his flesh, Aronofsky advertises that wrestling is a hustle, but that hustles have a cost and reality of their own. The quarry of *The Wrestler* is the real suffering of those with fake tans, the real bruises gained in the fixed match.

The fact that Randy looks like hell changes the viewer's relationship to Rourke's objectification. His face is withheld at the beginning of the film, creating a combination of desire and dread. Nothing about *9½ Weeks* had suggested that viewers should be uncomfortable looking at the gorgeous young Rourke. But in *The Wrestler*, when we see Randy being objectified or objectifying himself, we don't side with the gaze. When he goes for a beer with the exotic dancer Cassidy and she won't dance with him, he says 'fine then, I'll dance for you', and proceeds to mimic a lap dance. It's not sexy – it's just comically sad. When he has a one-night stand with a woman who dresses him up as a fireman, he wakes up in her apartment still wearing parts of the uniform. We share his self-loathing as he sneaks shamefully out, and it feels gross.

The Wrestler inverts the dynamic of the films that let women backstage to masculinity. If early in his career, Rourke's characters invited women to be male perverts, then his late characters invite men to be old whores. Randy's closeted transgenderism in *The Wrestler* can be usefully contrasted with the only 'out' performance of Rourke's thirty-year career. In *Animal Factory*, Rourke played 'Jan the Actress', the transgender bunk mate to Edward Furlong's posh young incarceree. The setting recalls *Bullet*, but with sexual alterity now foregrounded, not buried. We meet Jan as she lies on her bottom bunk filing her nails and fantasising. She has fashioned her linens into a set reminiscent of Nadar's portrait of Sarah Bernhardt, with voluminous white drapery, and she has movie-star pin-ups tacked to the walls. Jan has a Southern accent, a lisp and no front teeth, making her mouth a gaping hole when she laughs. In a Rourke-authored monologue, she drawls while reclining like an odalisque:

Rourke as 'Jan the Actress' in Steve Buscemi's
Animal Factory (2000)

I'll tell you something, when God put me together he made it fucked up,
he made a real bad mistake. I don't need this big old cock here, I'd just as soon
cut it off. The next lifetime, I'm just gonna be the girl next door. Let me tell
you something, if I had wings, I would be a butterfly and I would just fly out
the motherfucking window, I would fly across the ocean. You know where I'd
go? Where I've always wanted to go. I always wanted to go to Pawis, Fwance.
... I'd watch all the pretty Fwench boys walk by, and I would say, 'Hey you,
you go get Mama a café latte and a jelly donut, s'il vous plait.' And they would
wait on me and they would be polite to me and take me to pretty places.

It's the familiar Rourkean expression of desire for transcendence of
the body, for escape from the prison of the self, for multivalent and
counterintuitive identifications. And here, the emergence from the
closet does nothing to diminish Rourke's effects. As usual, he
discovers tensions and layers within Jan – sentimentality and
toughness, domesticity and sexual aggression – expressing these
visually in the contrast between her bulging muscular frame and her
delicate attire: red lace bra, false eyelashes, painted nails, belly-button

ring. In *The New York Times*, Elvis Mitchell noted that, despite Rourke's costuming, he doesn't 'overplay' the role, writing that his 'honeyed straightforwardness is more than just flirtatiousness' and that 'Rourke's verbal delicacy becomes part of his come on'.[23]

It's interesting that Rourke's Jan has the most vocal confidence of any of his characters. Jan's effort to derealise the materiality of gender, her self-fashioning as 'the Actress' and her cultivation of an identity of surplus, doubleness and paradox recall Rourke's first theatre role. When Genet's Green Eyes opens his shirt for his cell mates to reveal the tattoo of a woman's face beneath, he asks, 'I make a nice couple, eh?'[24] From *Deathwatch* to *The Wrestler*, this is the question that haunts all of Rourke's performances and defines his enigmatic merger of Method and camp: he was never just Stanley Kowalski, he was also Blanche DuBois. In the spectrum of sexual performance, he had now moved from the hustler, to the john and finally, in *Animal Factory*, to the queen.

4 ICON

His early promise was such that it galvanized an entire generation of young actors, making them want to do better, push harder, take more risks.

Sheila O'Malley, 'Gone Away, Come Back: Mickey Rourke'[1]

In the eighties, Mickey Rourke was the shit. If you were a young guy who loved movies and wanted to be an actor and was seeing a lot of movies in the eighties, there was nobody better than Mickey Rourke. De Niro, Pacino, Dustin Hoffman, they were all great, don't get me wrong. But Mickey Rourke was the man. I wanted to be Mickey Rourke.

James Gandolfini[2]

It's now three decades since Mickey Rourke first caught filmgoers' attention as the rock 'n' roll arsonist in *Body Heat*, and the 1980s are now a fixture of nostalgia culture. A revival of 1980s popular culture was a notable feature of the first decade of the twenty-first century, characterised by 'Eighties Nights', a return of fashion and music from the decade, and remakes of films like *Footloose* (1984) and *The Karate Kid* (1984). Currently, plans are in the works for a Broadway show based on Barry Levinson's *Diner*, with book by Levinson and music by Sheryl Crow, and *Vanity Fair* recently claimed that *Diner* was the most influential film of the past thirty years, because it 'caused a tectonic shift in popular culture. It paved the way for *Seinfeld*, *Pulp Fiction*, *The Office*, and Judd Apatow's career.'[3] As those who had been children and teenagers in the 1980s started to gain positions of power in the culture industry, they returned with affection to the objects of their youth – leg warmers, leather jackets, fingerless gloves, the music of Michael Jackson and Madonna. The children of the 1990s also discovered the culture they had never known the first time around, leading the vinyl revival and the adoption of 1980s styles. The emotional dynamics of this cultural return were captured in the 2007 film *Music and Lyrics*, featuring Hugh Grant as '80s has-been' Alex Fletcher. Fletcher described, from a fictional pop music icon's point of view, how it felt to reconnect with his fans at a reunion night after a long interlude: 'It was like I'd never been away. The audience was a tad older, as was I … but we were very, very happy to see each other again.' Grant's character had patented a signature dance move and set teenage girls' hearts fluttering in the early music video era. Capturing the bittersweet realities of this career, *Music and Lyrics* shows how, for an '80s has-been', surviving on the fringes of the entertainment industry required a strong work ethic, an ability to do behind-the-scenes jobs and most of all, some good-natured humility. Mickey Rourke did not seem interested in these things.

The 1980s revival was the second nostalgia trend that Rourke's career had passed through. A version of this had, in fact, happened in the 1980s, with a return of the popular culture of the 1950s. Rourke's early films were part of the diner-and-rock 'n' roll revival. *Diner* was set in 1959 and *Angel Heart* in 1955, while the black-and-white *Rumble Fish* harked back stylistically to the 'angry young man' films of the 1950s. More complicated in their relationship to the past than pure retro blockbusters like *Back to the Future* (1985), Rourke's films investigated the fault lines of the culture they depicted.[4] *Diner* exposed the sadness and frustration of a pre-sexual-revolution generation in which men and women had no idea how to talk to each other, while in *Angel Heart* Alan Parker complicated the iconography

Back to the diner: Rourke in *Angel Heart* (1987)

of the diner and Rourke's famous association with it from the earlier film by including a scene in which his character Harry Angel sits quietly at a diner counter after investigating a witness.

Reconstructing the film's events in light of the knowledge, gleaned later, that it was Angel himself who murdered all the witnesses, we realise that this diner interlude was the period in which Angel was committing his acts of violence. Parker uses the diner as the space for a kind of purgatorial lull – not a realistic stretch of action at all, but a visual pause to indicate the time during which Angel was wreaking his violence. In Parker's film, as in *Diner* and *The Wrestler*, Rourke becomes an embodiment of a complicated nostalgia – a yearning for the past, accompanied by an acknowledgment that the past is not an escape from the present but the time when the conditions of the present were shaped.

Just as Rourke had inhabited a grittier 1980s than the likes of Wham!, Michael J. Fox and the Brat Pack, in recent years he has represented a grittier form of nostalgia. *The Wrestler* begins with

From the opening credits of *The Wrestler*
(2008): recalling Randy's glory days in the ring

shots of press clippings from Randy the Ram's wrestling glory days, accompanied by that era's heavy metal music. Aronofsky's film is more complicated than a mere celebration of Randy's youth. In the film's present, Randy is one step away from living in the van that is wallpapered on the inside with the clips and glossy photos of his youth, now exposed as the tattered remains of his narcissism. The cost of the years Randy spent on the road, away from his daughter, and abusing his body in the name of money, fame and strength, is clear to see. Equally apparent – in the rematches with his old opponent 'The Ayatollah' – are the continuing geopolitics of the period since the 1980s.[5] Whereas most retro culture is simply an effort to connect to the feel-good parts of the past, Aronofsky exposes Randy's nostalgia and his values as a decades-old tragedy.

It wasn't until the 1980s had cycled back into fashion – and until he had started to mend some of the bridges he had burned in Hollywood – that Rourke could enter a new phase of his career. He started turning up again in a series of high-profile cameos around the turn of the century – first in Francis Ford Coppola's *The Rainmaker*, then in Vincent Gallo's *Buffalo '66* (1998), next in Sean Penn's *The Pledge* and finally, in Robert Rodriguez's *Once Upon a Time in Mexico* (2003) and Frank Miller's *Sin City*. Most of the comeback artists of the same moment – Robert Downey Jr, Charlie Sheen, Alec Baldwin – still looked relatively vital. Though their second act careers were subject to some modification (moving to comedy from romantic leads, for instance), they could mostly just pick up where they left off, with minor capitulations to middle age. Other 1980s survivors might have encouraged the idea that their hard-living youth hadn't taken a serious toll (Slash of Guns N' Roses was now a family man and the face of the *Guitar Center* franchise, while Jon Bon Jovi was running a soup kitchen in New Jersey), but Rourke's face registered the cost of his wilderness years. It also finally allowed him to become what he had always really been – a character actor.

In his comeback performances at the turn of the century, Rourke was doing what he had done the first time around in Hollywood – moving audiences and getting noticed in small parts. Only this time he was doing it with *that* face, scarred by boxing and botched plastic surgery in a way no make-up or filters could disguise. To show such a face was a new form of compelling vulnerability. Those who had loved him in their youths, who had followed him from one film to the next with suspense, were moved anew by his power on screen, and started to talk about what he had meant to them thirty years earlier. Mourning for Rourke's former looks existed alongside admiration for, and curiosity about, a talent that could hold the screen without them. A *New York Times* profile of November 2008 dwelled on the loss of the original star and the birth of a new one:

He has lost his soft, fragile beauty. Filmgoers won't see him in *The Wrestler* and flash back to his other films. In Rourke's third act, he is literally a new face and a new actor. He has lost the tics that were once a sign of an original talent, then later a kind of posturing. The sly, sensitive smile with a hint of sex and menace. The languid gestures, the touching of his face and hair (always tortured into a '50s pompadour), as if he were caressing himself. The mumbled lines that suggested sensitivity. Today his elusive, almost feminine presence is gone.[6]

There was certainly nothing pretty about his character's face in *Sin City*, the 2005 film that brought him back into the spotlight. *Sin City* was 'practically a homecoming' for Rourke, said Mick LaSalle in the *San Francisco Chronicle*, and indeed, though playing a comic-book character, Rourke's costume alluded to his realist roots: he sported the time-tested Actors Studio uniform of white undershirt and gold chain, just as he had in *The Pope of Greenwich Village*.[7] Rourke seemed to be entering his legacy period, finally ready to do what was required to secure a lasting place in Hollywood. *Sin City* and *Iron Man 2* were smart career moves, allowing him to take his place alongside his generational peers (Bruce Willis, Robert Downey Jr), while simultaneously introducing him to a large audience of enthusiastic young viewers. Both films were based on comics and were tied to large markets that promoted extra-cinematic products (*Sin City*'s line of merchandise included an action figure called 'Death Row Marv', based on Rourke's character). A glance at his filmography reminds us that Rourke had long been attracted to pulpy parts (*Angel Heart*, *Johnny Handsome*, *9½ Weeks* and *The Last Ride* inhabited the genres of hard-boiled, B-movie, softcore and Western, respectively). But the change was in the prominence of the venues – in a reversal of Norma Desmond's fate, it was the movies that got big: these were blockbusters of the sort Rourke had never performed in. He was now in pulp in a commercially successful way, and he was acting up a storm.

In *Sin City*, Rourke dominated the screen for approximately twenty minutes as the narrator and protagonist of a section called 'The Hard Goodbye'. He played a beastly tough guy avenging the death of a prostitute beauty named Goldie with whom he had shared one night of love. It was classic Rourke territory. 'Mickey Rourke gives a sensational comeback performance as Marv', wrote Peter Travers in *Rolling Stone*,[8] while Frank Miller, the originator of the *Sin City* series, was blown away, declaring 'Mickey IS Marv'.

Marv in Frank Miller's *Sin City* (2005)

Mick LaSalle from the *San Francisco Chronicle* singled him out from the cast for his stellar performance:

Here's an actor who has seemed a bit strange in any cinematic setting for at least ten years. But in this comic book context of outsized villains and heroes, everything grand-scale and skewed about Rourke as a screen presence becomes a virtue. It's not enough to say that Rourke is good in *Sin City*. It really feels like he lives there.[9]

While they were lauding his acting, critics were also scrambling for prose that could capture Marv's haggard appearance. 'He looks like a chunk of granite abandoned by a sculptor,' remarked one, and the attempts multiplied: his 'bandaged face … comes to resemble a granite cliff that a flock of gulls has smacked into'; 'a face like roadkill'; 'the plug-ugly, psychopathically violent Marv, who resembles a centaur walking on two feet' with 'a Frankenstein jaw line'.[10] With his extravagantly bandaged face, Marv looked like the walking wound that he was.

Critics and audiences couldn't get enough of this brilliant crystallisation and update of the Rourke persona – a 'two-time loser' and denizen of raunchy saloons who had both a penchant for violent slayings and the purest of hearts. The story was told in black and white, with Rourke's gruff voice supplying the voiceover in perfect noir style. Rourke stole the film and won a string of awards for the performance. As one might expect from such cinephiles as Robert Rodriguez and his co-directors, Frank Miller and Quentin Tarantino, *Sin City* provided a meta-reflection on Rourke's particular combination of noir hero and method actor, and a rearrangement of his career themes around his current age and looks. The film's directors understood – as Aronofsky also did – that the older Rourke's career would thrive best if it was less a renunciation than a recalibration of the old Rourke themes. How do you manage the persona of a sex symbol once he has ceased to look like a sex symbol? The danger would be casting Rourke implausibly as a leading man. His role as Marv in *Sin City* was an anthology of favoured sexual outlaw motifs, made epic by the cinematography and the distance provided by Rourke's voiceover. 'The night's as hot as hell,' Rourke's narrative began: 'It's a lousy room in a lousy part of a lousy town. I'm staring at a goddess. She's telling me she wants me. I'm not going to waste one more second wondering how I've gotten so lucky.' Here is the new Rourke persona: as attentive to women as he was in *Diner*, but now genuinely and plausibly mystified by the miracle of returned affection.

* * *

After the popular and critical triumphs of *Sin City* and *The Wrestler*, Rourke seemed to lose his way once more. Mitch Glazer's *Passion*

Play (2010) – 'a wildly surreal western fantasy' – was given a very limited release.[11] The reason? 'If the degree of laughter at the wrong moments and the number of walkouts at the Toronto International Film Festival are any indication, the film will appeal only to the most fondly indulgent.'[12] Even Rourke told journalists it was a terrible movie, and then, as usual, apologised. With echoes of the reviews for *Wild Orchid*, critics called it a 'self-indulgent sexual fantasy run amok' and delivered the verdict that 'Rourke and [Megan] Fox are a thoroughly mismatched screen couple, who exude zero screen chemistry with one another'.[13] For *Time Out*, it was 'a swooningly pretentious piece of carnival drama'.[14] The disaster prompted critics, once again, to reconsider Rourke's viability as a star. Some conceded that his 'rumpled hard-man vulnerability is part of his charm and fans will enjoy his work', while others felt that he 'possesses a down and out shaggy dog appeal that only works in a very limited, realistic range of films'.[15] The 'trashy' accusations from the *Wild Orchid* days reasserted themselves in *Time Out*'s verdict: 'You can take the phoenix-rising actor out of straight-to-video trash, but – well, you know the rest of it.'[16] But even a flop like *Passion Play* shows the constellation of interests that makes Rourke so compelling. The fetishism, the way women's bodies are presented as connected to – and keys to – male melancholia and feelings of dysphoria, as well as Rourke's alternative spirit, his celebration of that which lies beyond the norm: in this case, quite literally, a sideshow aesthetic. When Megan Fox's character Lily Luster decides to get plastic surgery to remove the wings that have made her career in a carnival freak show, Nate (Rourke) urges her to change her mind: 'Please don't do this,' he begs, and when she pleads that she'd like to be like everybody else, he tells her, 'Fuck normal.' It's another of Rourke's plastic surgery fables, and this time he comes down on the side of accepting one's body in its natural state. The film ends with Lily flying away with Nate gathered up in her arms. It's deeply weird. But it's also a cinematic moment that

To save and be saved by a woman: Rourke and
Megan Fox in *Passion Play* (2010)

suitably registers the recurrent desire of Rourke's characters to save
and be saved by a woman.

At times, the casting of Rourke in this late phase of his career
still seems to have one foot stubbornly in the 1980s. To see him
playing opposite Megan Fox in *Passion Play* requires either the
suspension of disbelief or a very good memory of the young Rourke.
Hollywood has never shied away from casting older male stars as
lovers to much younger women (Fred Astaire and Audrey Hepburn
in *Funny Face* [1957], Bill Murray and Scarlett Johansson in *Lost in
Translation* [2003]), but Rourke's weathered appearance makes such
casting more than usually implausible. Rourke's recent films must
find some way to acknowledge his changed appearance. In *Passion
Play*, Megan Fox's character brings up the past and thus gives us a
fighting chance to justify Rourke as love object in this film, as she
asks out loud what the audience might be thinking: 'You were
famous, handsome. What happened?' Former fame is also used to
justify his relationship with Cassidy (Marisa Tomei) in *The Wrestler*,
while the Rourke storyline in *Sin City* is styled as a fable located far
outside the bounds of realism. In Tony Scott's *Domino* (2005), the
problem of reconciling the new Rourke with his old sex-and-sleaze
image is solved in two ways: first, by having his character Ed reflect

on his wild 1980s past (including an allusion to an affair with Pat Benatar), and second, by casting him in a threesome as a team of bounty hunters with Keira Knightley and Edgar Ramirez (both men are depicted as desiring Knightley, but Ramirez ends up her love object, while Knightley's character calls Ed 'My boss, my mentor, the father I never had'). Playing a mentor figure had always worked well for Rourke – it was what he had done even at his peak opposite Colette Blonigan as Carole Heathrow in *Diner* and Kim Basinger in *9½ Weeks*. In *Domino*, he reluctantly agrees to let a 'delicate thing' like Domino Harvey into the dangerous business of bounty hunting, and comes to value her toughness, again playing the sensation-seeking woman's guide to life on the edge.

This role also became part of Rourke's image in popular culture. He was everyone's favourite wild one. When Evan Rachel Wood (who played Rourke's daughter in *The Wrestler*) told journalists that Rourke had given her a cake for her twenty-first birthday and included handcuffs in the box, she added, 'He knows me so well. By the end of the night, I was handcuffed to a champagne bottle and didn't know what happened.'[17] Tina Fey's sitcom *30 Rock* included a running Mickey Rourke joke, always delivered by the show's diva character Jenna Maroney, who would confess her kinky adventures with Rourke. When chastising a co-worker for his incompetence, for instance, Maroney tells him: 'I'm going to have to reinvent you, break you down completely and build you up from scratch, just like Mickey Rourke did to me sexually.' Or, on another occasion, she threatens: 'You know what they say, boys: If you can't stand the heat, get off of Mickey Rourke's sex grill!' Here, Rourke provides a reference point for that which is even kinkier than the show's kinkiest character. Another spin on Rourkean kink appeared in the reimagining of his *9½ Weeks* character for Jon Favreau's *Iron Man 2*. As the villain Whiplash, Rourke's hands are transformed into whips, his body contained in painful-looking wire contraptions. He isn't just into SM, he *is* SM.

Jon Favreau's *Iron Man 2* (2010)

In the unusual way that Rourke has blended a career as a sex symbol with a reputation for greatness as an actor, his star status recalls Marlon Brando's. In a 2008 article titled 'Shades of Brando', Will Leitch compares the careers of both actors, finding echoes everywhere. Phase 1: *On the Waterfront* ('clearly he's a contendah' – *Body Heat*, *Diner*, *Rumble Fish*); Phase 2: *Last Tango in Paris* (1972) ('soft porn' – *9½ Weeks*, *Wild Orchid*); Phase 3: *The Island of Dr Moreau* (1996) ('the lost decade' – *Harley Davidson and the Marlboro Man*); Phase 4: *Apocalypse Now* (1979) ('late-blooming, defeated anger' – *Sin City*); Phase 5: *The Godfather* (1972) ('for the first time in years, the movie is as good as he is' – *The Wrestler*).[18] Sheila O'Malley also compares Rourke to Brando, 'in terms of the *level of the gift* – so far and beyond what his peers are bringing to the table'. She calls Rourke 'Brando-ish in his inventive-ness, his freedom, his specificity', but she also compares him to Brando in the way that he handled his talent: 'These men are so gifted that they are careless with that gift.[19] If Rourke resembles Brando in his magnetism, his career trajectory and his acting style, he does not share Brando's earthy sexuality or his comfort with taking public intellectual and political positions. In these ways, Rourke is still closer to Montgomery Clift, a fellow artist of yearnings and sufferings who portrays characters always on the threshold of a revelation that never comes. His career also resembles Clift's in the way that his face changed dramatically: Brando, like Elvis Presley, just got older and rounder, forcing his fans to face their own middle age, but Clift's face, like Rourke's after boxing and plastic surgery, was notably different after his car accident, and forced him to start a second, distinct phase of his career as a star.

Though his image is still primarily that of a Method actor, now that he has the gravitas of old age, Rourke has recently flirted with the status of the classical actor, too. He's been turning up in some parts you might expect from Laurence Olivier in his *Clash of the Titans* (1981) period, such as his role as the Greek god Hyperion in *Immortals* (2011). These days, his theatricality is as extravagant as it ever was, and in his role as Whiplash in *Iron Man 2*, Rourke is positively camp. Here is Peter Travers relishing the excesses of Rourke's performance:

Ha! Enter Ivan Vanko, a.k.a. Whiplash, a Russian killing machine played by Mickey Rourke like his *Wrestler* character after a massive case of tattoo poisoning. Rourke is a bloody wonder, spitting out his lines in an outrageous Russian accent to rival John Malkovich in *Rounders*. To hear Vanko pine for his parrot ('*Vere eees my boird?*') is comic bliss. Rourke, too good an actor to slide by on silliness, invests Vanko with human dimensions. Hardened by his time in prison, he blames Stark for the death of his father and for stealing his invention … Rourke is more than enough of an adversary for one movie.[20]

Roger Ebert also registered the enjoyable excess: 'Mickey Rourke gives us all the Ivan Vanko we could possibly wish for, unless he had a third arm to provide space for more tattoos.'[21] There was a grand theatricality to Rourke's performance in *Sin City*, too, though this was in a more serious vein. He inhabited the role of Marv as a pulp Hamlet, weighing the moral stakes of his revenge and asking, with angst, 'What if I've imagined all of this ... Can't kill a man without knowing for sure you ought to, I've got to know for sure.'

⋆ ⋆ ⋆

Rourke's eclectic career spans four decades, from the late-1970s era of Cimino and Coppola to the present. As a young star, Rourke reinvigorated but also questioned the erotic power of suffering Method masculinity, using his gestural performance style, his connections to the worlds of sport and rock music, and his investigations of gender and sexuality to forge a distinctive but tenuous place as a blue-collar virtuoso and self-styled industry outsider. The later Rourke, like Dennis Hopper, became a muse to a new generation of independent film-makers, returning to prove himself as a phenomenally moving older actor. Despite the long misunderstanding between this talented actor and the Hollywood film industry, occasionally Rourke and Hollywood come together and he gives a mesmerising, iconic, highly adulated performance, one that he then consistently refuses to parlay into a steady career in the film establishment. Rourke's take-it-or-leave-it attitude towards stardom seems to account for his popularity with certain indie-minded directors, from Vincent Gallo to Robert Rodriguez to Darren Aronofsky. He is the perfect hipster fetish, especially for the early twenty-first century, when hipsterdom came to be defined by an interest in the accoutrements of working-class whiteness: 'trucker hats; undershirts called "wifebeaters," worn alone; the aesthetic of basement rec-room pornography, flash-lit Polaroids, and fake-wood paneling; Pabst Blue Ribbon; "porno" or "pedophile" mustaches; aviator glasses; ... the late albums of

Johnny Cash; tattoos'.[22] Darren Aronofsky was keen to cast Rourke in *The Wrestler* because he is 'a legitimate working-class guy, which is unusual in a leading man'.[23] Perhaps it was simply inevitable that Rourke, like Johnny Cash – a talented artist who proudly bore the marks of his humble origins – should come to be treasured in this way. As Aronofsky retailed the story of his difficulties raising funds on Mickey Rourke's name, it was clear that Rourke had become the muse of independent film directors: to cast him was to indicate one's faith in art over and above the 'suits' who ran the film industry – or, as Randy called them in *The Wrestler*, 'the guys with the Cadillacs'.

Even beyond this cultural currency, there's always something indie in spirit about Rourke's acting. In his pacing (and this is especially evident when he's not in the leading role), Rourke tends to inhabit movies differently than his co-stars. He is on his own wavelength, 'alternative' in his performances, even in mainstream films. Consider *The Expendables*, Sylvester Stallone's 2010 film that features an ensemble cast of action stars (Stallone, Jet Li, Jason Statham, etc.). Rourke plays a tattoo artist, the only cast member not caught up in action-film masculinity. He wants to die in a woman's arms. His major monologue reflects on a moral crisis and the loss of his soul. Mick LaSalle noticed the same feature in his performance as Marv in *Sin City*, writing that Rourke seems 'confident and bizarre and with a strange imperviousness, as though not occupying the same reality as everyone else'.[24] Or, as Cintra Wilson described his performance in *Diner*, 'all the other actors are on a chatty 78 rpm and Rourke is on a self-consciously heavy 33'.[25]

These days, Rourke is at work trying to raise funds for a biopic based on the life of the first openly gay Welsh rugby player, Gareth Thomas. If it gets made, the film will be something of a sequel to Rourke's 1988 film *Homeboy*, and one that will pay tribute to an athlete who prevailed over the immense taboo against homosexuality in professional sports to come out publicly. But aside from this promising project, nothing Rourke has done since *The Wrestler* seems quite worthy of his talent. Pauline Kael is no longer with us to comment on the winter of Rourke's career, but her remarks on the later roles of Brando come to mind when one watches *Iron Man 2*: 'when he appears on the screen, there is a special quality of recognition in the audience: we know he's too big for the role'.[26] Indeed, Rourke's characters have never quite fit into their bodies or their social roles or their families or their moment in history. Watching them negotiate such feelings, trying to express everything that lies beyond what a Hollywood script can say about class, gender and sexuality, has generated three decades' worth of compelling viewing. The best of Rourke's performances – in *Diner*, *Rumble Fish*, *The Pope of Greenwich Village*, *9½ Weeks*, *Barfly*, *Angel Heart*, *Homeboy*, *Johnny Handsome*, *Sin City* and *The Wrestler* – add up to a moving, vulnerable, masterful body of work, one with analogues in Brando and Clift, but also one that is as idiosyncratic and fascinatingly scarred as Mickey Rourke himself.

NOTES

Introduction

1 Deborah Ross, 'The Outsider', *Independent*, 1 December 2003.

2 Pauline Kael, '*Diner*', in *For Keeps* (New York: Plume, 1996), p. 931.

3 There are two book-length accounts of Mickey Rourke's life: Sandra Monetti, *Mickey Rourke: Wrestling with Demons* (Montreal: Transit Publishing, 2010), and Christopher Heard, *Mickey Rourke: High and Low* (London: Plexus Publishing, 2006).

4 Pat Jordan, 'His Fists Are Up and His Guard Is Down', *New York Times*, 28 November 2008.

5 Steve Garbarino, 'The Resurrection of Mickey Rourke', *Maxim Magazine*, December 2008.

1 Method actor

1 Richard Dyer, 'Coming Out as Going In: The Image of the Homosexual as a Sad Young Man', in *The Culture of Queers* (New York: Routledge, 2001), pp. 116–36.

2 Vincent Canby, 'A Feast of Interesting, Original New Work', *New York Times*, 11 April 1982.

3 Krista Smith, 'Q & A: Mitch Glazer on Megan Fox, Mickey Rourke, and His New Miami Gangster Series', *Vanity Fair*, 6 May 2011.

4   Steve Vineberg, *Method Actors: Three Generations of an American Acting Style* (New York: Schirmer Trade Books, 1994), p. xxi.

5   Ibid.

6   Konstantin Stanislavski, *An Actor's Work: A Student's Diary*, trans. Jean Benedetti (New York: Routledge, 2008), p. 209.

7   Sandra Seacat, quoted in Robert Walden, 'The Method and the Myth', *Backstage*, 21 April 2009.

8   Stanislavski, *An Actor's Work*, p. 196.

9   *Inside the Actors Studio*: 'Mickey Rourke'. Hosted by James Lipton. Broadcast 31 August 2009.

10   Janet Maslin, 'Scavenging to Make New Movies', *New York Times*, 13 September 1981.

11   Vincent Canby, 'For American Movies, a Minor Renaissance', *New York Times*, 27 December 1981.

12   Robert Hatch, *The Nation*, 24 April 1982.

13   John Simon, 'Genre: And a Bit Beyond', *The National Review*, 14 May 1982, p. 572.

14   Canby, 'A Feast of Interesting, Original New Work'.

15   Francis Ford Coppola, quoted in Roger Ebert, '*Rumble Fish*', *Chicago Sun-Times*, 26 August 1983.

16   Ebert, '*Rumble Fish*'.

17   S. E. Hinton, *Rumble Fish* (New York: Laurel Leaf, 1989), p. 27.

18   Ibid., p. 33.

19   Maslin continues: 'With his hair cut oddly so that the hairline suggests a heart, and with a gentle intelligence that transcends even the silliest lines … he does an outstanding job.' Janet Maslin, '*Rumble Fish* (1983)', *New York Times*, 7 October 1983.

20   Elia Kazan, quoted in Vineberg, *Method Actors*, p. 107.

21   Cintra Wilson, 'Mickey Rourke's Desperate Truths', *Salon*, 15 May 2002. Available at: http://www.salon.com/2002/15/rourke.

2 Softcore star

1 Alessandra Stanley, 'Can 50 Million Frenchmen Be Wrong?', *New York Times*, 21 October 1990.

2 Sheila Benson, '"Dragon": A Compelling Look Inside Chinatown', *LA Times*, 16 August 1985.

3 Pauline Kael, '*Diner*', in *For Keeps* (New York: E. P. Dutton, 1994), p. 931.

4 Richard Mahler, 'On the Set: On "The Last Outlaw's" Trail: HBO Shoots 'Em Up in New Mexico', *LA Times*, 24 October 1993.

5 Sophie Morris, 'Mickey Rourke: The Bruiser Is Back', *Independent*, 3 January 2009.

6 Rita Kempley, '*Angel Heart*', *Washington Post*, 6 March 1987.

7 Kent Williams, 'The Wrestler: Mickey Rourke Toughens Up', *Isthmus*, 16 January 2009.

8 Cintra Wilson, 'Mickey Rourke's Desperate Truths', *Salon*, 15 May 2002. Available at: http://www.salon.com/2002/15/rourke.

9 Sheila O'Malley, 'Through the Fishtank: Mickey Rourke in *The Rainmaker*', *The Sheila Variations*, 27 December 2008. Available at: http://www.sheilaomalley.com/?p=8730.

10 Kael, '*Diner*', p. 931.

11 Linda Williams, 'Studying Soft Sex', *Film Quarterly* vol. 62 no. 1, 2008, p. 86.

12 Sheila Benson, 'Masochistic Love Affair in "9½ Weeks"', *LA Times*, 21 February 1986.

13 Jay Boyar, '*9½ Weeks*', *Orlando Sentinel*, 19 April 1986.

14 *Montreal Gazette*, 15 March 1986.

15 Vincent Canby, '"9½ Weeks," a Sexual Journey', *New York Times*, 21 February 1986.

16 Tom Matthews, '*9½ Weeks*', *Boxoffice*, 1 April 1986.

17 Canby, '"9½ Weeks"'.

18 Ibid.

19 Mark Morris, '9½ Weeks', *Observer*, 4 May 1990.

20 Benson, 'Masochistic Love Affair'.

21 Candice Russell, 'Steamy Saga Nothing but a Tease', *Fort Lauderdale Sun Sentinel*, 21 April 1986.

22 Jeff Millar, '*9½ Weeks*', *Houston Chronicle*, 18 April 1986.

23 Christopher Harris, '9½ Weeks', *Ottawa Citizen*, 5 April 1988.

24 *Montreal Gazette*, 15 March 1986.

25 Michael Janusosis, *Providence Journal*, 1986.

26 Jay Scott, '9½ Weeks', *Globe and Mail*, 21 February 1986.

27 *9½ Weeks* appeared just before the period that saw the mainstreaming of kink and the release of an increasing number of popular culture products that treated bondage, domination and sadomasochism in a new way, as domesticated, non-threatening and appealing to a broader spectrum of people. Margot D. Weiss cites such films as *Exit to Eden* (1994), *Quills* (2000) and *Secretary* (2002) as evidence that the practices of kink were gaining a new kind of mainstream exposure and acceptability. Margot D. Weiss, 'Mainstreaming Kink: The Politics of Popular BDSM Representation in U.S. Popular Media', *Journal of Homosexuality* vol. 50 no. 2–3, pp. 103–30.

28 David Andrews, *Soft in the Middle: The Contemporary Softcore Feature in Its Contexts* (Columbus: Ohio State University Press, 2006), pp. 391, 392.

29 Russell, 'Steamy Saga Nothing but a Tease'.

30 Nancy Collins, '"Sex Slave" Kim Leads a Quiet Life', *Toronto Star*, 13 April 1986.

31 Miriam Hansen identifies these features in *The Sheik*, as well as the 'oscillation of the Valentino persona between sadistic and masochistic positions'. Miriam Hansen, 'Pleasure, Ambivalence, Identification: Valentino and Female Spectatorship', in Leo Braudy and Marshall Cohen (eds), *Film Theory and Criticism* (New York: OUP, 2004; first published 1974), pp. 643–4.

32 Elizabeth McNeill, *Nine and a Half Weeks: A Memoir of a Love Affair* (New York: E. P. Dutton, 1978; reprint 2005).

33 Stanley, 'Can 50 Million Frenchmen Be Wrong?'

34 Leslie Adrienne Miller, *Mississippi Review* vol. 27 no. 1–2, 1998, pp. 14–15.

35 'Mickey Rourke's career plummet ... can be traced to his work in softcore sex films,' writes Linda Ruth Williams in *The Erotic Thriller in Contemporary Cinema*, noting how many of his films 'have strong softcore elements running through them which sexualize Rourke (though he is seldom a beefcake equivalent of the female cheesecake), making him a fascinating figure for discussions of contemporary masculinity and performance, shot through with an existential aloofness.' Linda Ruth Williams, *The Erotic Thriller in Contemporary Cinema* (Bloomington: Indiana University Press, 2005), p. 148.

36 Mickey Rourke, quoted in Carré Otis and Hugo Schwyzer, *Beauty, Disrupted: A Memoir* (New York: HarperCollins It Books, 2011), p. 162.

37 Susan Sontag, 'Notes on Camp', in *Against Interpretation* (New York: Picador, 1966), p. 291.

38 Vincent Canby, 'Angel Heart', *New York Times*, 6 March 1987.

39 Roger Ebert, 'Angel Heart', *Chicago Sun-Times*, 6 March 1987.

40 Rita Kempley, '*Angel Heart*', *Washington Post*, 6 March 1987.

41 Parker has often been criticised for the way his films fictionalise or aestheticise complex political terrains. In the case of *Mississippi Burning*, which treats the murder of three civil rights workers in Mississippi, *The New York Times* asked one of their reporters who had covered the civil rights movement, rather than a film critic, to comment on the film. Parker's *Evita* (1997), based on Andrew Lloyd Webber's musical about the career of Argentina's Eva Peron, also stylised painful historical territory.

42 Canby, 'Angel Heart'.

43 Ebert, 'Angel Heart'.

44 Jonathan Rosenbaum, 'Barfly', *Chicago Reader*, n.d.

45 Charles Bukowski, *Hollywood* (New York: Ecco, 2002; first published 1989), p. 148.

46 David Andrews provides a detailed reading of Rourke's performances in *9½ Weeks* and *Wild Orchid*, calling Rourke the epitome of Zalman King's 'low hero'. He writes that: 'King's low male hero is complex and has elaborately gendered narrative functions. The main function of King's low male is to serve as his heroine's heterosexual object, with his literal sex

following from this role. But his secondary function is to register the heroine's new assertiveness, which proceeds from the hero's erotic effect. On her sexual "awakening," she grows more masculinized as he grows more feminized; in a sense, he causes his own emasculation. These shifts in the hero's secondary function are reinforced by shifts in the meaning of his class position. At the start, the hero's abjection signifies his raw machismo, which simultaneously agitates the heroine and controls her. At the end, his low status accentuates an emotional vulnerability with a socioeconomic context. Thus, by the conclusion, the domesticated hero resembles a traditional romance heroine, implying the heroine's ambivalent elevation to hero status.' Andrews, *Soft in the Middle*, p. 116.

47 Otis and Schwyzer, *Beauty, Disrupted*, p. 130.
48 Ibid., pp. 132, 142.

3 Fighter

1 Levinson, quoted in Stephanie Zacharek, 'Here's Looking at You, Comeback Kids', *Salon*, 20 February 2009. Available at: http://www.salon.com/2009/02/20/rourke_downey/.

2 Rourke's mutability was powerful on screen, but it became a problem on set. Not everyone liked to work with him, perhaps because when he wasn't being intimate and generous, he seemed capable of breaking the spirits of other actors with his quick mood changes and unpredictable improvisations. Kim Basinger found him problematic and even threatening. Alan Parker said of *Angel Heart*, 'working with Mickey is a nightmare. He is very dangerous on set because you never know what he's going to do.'

3 In the wake of Rourke's comeback in *The Wrestler*, Ratner edited this footage into a short film called *Meet Mickey Rourke*, clearly with an allusion to Albert and David Maysles's 1966 film *Meet Marlon Brando*. The film was released as part of Ratner's *Shooter Series* in 2009.

4 Scott Raab, 'Mickey Rourke', *Real Hollywood Stories* (Boulder, CO: Tatra, 2008), p. 198.

5   Rourke's pen name as a screenwriter was 'Sir Eddie Cook'. He borrowed
    the name 'Eddie Cook' from Sidney Poitier's character – an expat jazz
    musician – in Martin Ritt's *Paris Blues* (1961). The knighthood he
    apparently supplied himself.

6   Cintra Wilson, 'Mickey Rourke's Desperate Truths', *Salon*, 15 May 2002.
    Available at: http://www.salon.com/2002/15/rourke.

7   Bob Dylan, *Chronicles: Volume One* (New York: Simon and Schuster,
    2005), p. 213.

8   Roland Barthes, 'The World of Wrestling', in *Mythologies*, trans. Annette
    Lavers (New York: Farrar, Straus and Giroux, 1972), p. 16.

9   Darren Aronofsky, quoted in Sheila Johnston, 'Mickey Rourke Bounces
    Back off the Ropes', *Telegraph*, 2 January 2009.

10 Anthony Lane, '*The Wrestler*', *New Yorker*, 22 December 2008.

11 Amy Biacolli, '*The Wrestler*', *Houston Chronicle*, 15 January 2009.

12 Rene Rodriguez, '*The Wrestler*', *Miami Herald*, n.d.

13 Tom Huddleston, '*The Wrestler*', *Time Out London*, 15–24 January 2009.

14 Peter Bradshaw, '*The Wrestler*', *Guardian*, 15 January 2009.

15 Roger Ebert, '*The Wrestler*', *Chicago Sun-Times*, 23 December 2008.

16 Kenneth Turan, 'As Fake as Wrestling', *LA Times*, 17 December 2008.

17 'International Man of the Year: Mickey Rourke', *GQ*, January 2009.

18 Grant Japhy, 'Mickey Rourke Super Sorry He's a Homophobic Asshole',
    Queerty, 11 November 2008. Available at: http://www.queerty.com/
    mickey-rourke-sorry-hes-a-homophobic-asshole-20081111/.

19 David Savran, *Taking It Like a Man: White Masculinity, Masochism, and
    Contemporary American Culture* (Princeton, NJ: Princeton University
    Press, 2008).

20 Darren Aronofsky, quoted by Mickey Rourke in Jonathan Crocker,
    '*The Wrestler*: Rourke Gets Real in Aronofsky's Stripped-Down
    Bodyslammer', *Total Film: The Guide to Modern Movies*, 28 April 2009.

21 Seth Abramovitch, 'Parents Outraged as Annie Leibovitz Sexualizes
    Mickey Rourke for Her Art', *Defamer*, 4 February 2009. Available at:
    http://gawker.com/5146339/parents-outraged-as-annie-leibovitz-
    sexualizes-mickey-rourke-for-her-art.

22 Raab, 'Mickey Rourke', p. 190.

23 Elvis Mitchell, 'Surviving the Lockup One Way or Another', *New York Times*, 20 October 2000.

24 Jean Genet, *The Maids and Deathwatch* (New York: Grove, 1994), p. 125.

4 Icon

1 Sheila O'Malley, 'Gone Away, Come Back: Mickey Rourke', *Slant*, 17 December 2008. Available at: http://www.slantmagazine.com/house/2008/17/gone-away-come-back-mickey-rourke.

2 James Gandolfini, quoted in Matt Zoller Seitz, 'James Gandolfini, 1961–2013: A Great Actor, A Better Man', *Vulture*, 20 June 2013. Available at: http://www.vulture.com/2013/06/james-gandolfini-obit-matt-zoller-seitz.htm.

3 S. L. Price, 'Much Ado about Nothing: How Barry Levinson's *Diner* Changed Cinema, 30 Years Later', *Vanity Fair*, March 2012.

4 Stephen Prince has argued that *Back to the Future* 'epitomized the collective yearning for a pristine past that the Reagan years had defined as a core national aspiration' (Prince, quoted in Andrew Shail and Robin Stoate, *Back to the Future* [London: BFI, 2010]); and Andrew Shail and Robin Stoate define the film's 'Reaganite nostalgia' more fully as 'a yearning for certain supposedly decayed ideals – such small-town, post-war values of the Eisenhower era as childhood innocence, the nuclear family and the domestic American dream … The film's treatment of the past strongly positions the 1950s as a lost object of desire' (Stoate and Shail, *Back to the Future*, p. 50).

5 *The Guardian* reported in December 2008 that members of the Iranian media had lodged complaints against the scene in which Randy breaks the pole of an Iranian flag over his knee before defeating 'The Ayatollah' to the sounds of a crowd chanting 'USA!' (Robert Tait, 'Hollywood Film Accused of Insulting Iran', *Guardian*, 12 December 2008.)

6   Pat Jordan, 'His Fists Are Up, and His Guard Is Down', *New York Times*, 28 November 2008.

7   Mick LaSalle, '*Sin City*', *San Francisco Chronicle*, 1 April 2005.

8   Peter Travers, '*Sin City*', *Rolling Stone*, 1 April 2005.

9   LaSalle, '*Sin City*'.

10 Ken Tucker, 'Sin City', *New York Magazine*, 21 May 2005; 'B.W.', 'Sin City', *Time Out London*, no. 1815, 1–8 June 2005; Manohla Dargis, 'Sin City', *New York Times*, 1 April 2005; Philip French, 'Sin City', *Observer*, 4 June 2005; Travers, 'Sin City'.

11 Eric Kohn, 'Megan Fox, Mickey Rourke and Bill Murray Lose Direction in Awful "Passion Play"', *Indiewire*, 3 May 2011. Available at: http://www.indiewire.com/article/review_megan_fox_mickey_rourke_and_bill_murray_lose_direction_in_awful_pass.

12 Ray Bennett, 'Passion Play', *Hollywood Reporter*, 14 October 2010.

13 Jeremy Heilman, 'Passion Play', *Moviemartyr.com*, 14 July 2011. Available at: http://www.moviemartyr.com/2010/passionplay.htm.

14 Joshua Rothkopf, 'Passion Play', *Time Out*, 3 May 2011.

15 Kohn, 'Awful *Passion Play*'; Bennett, 'Passion Play'.

16 Rothkopf, 'Passion Play'.

17 Steve Garbarino, 'The Resurrection of Mickey Rourke', *Maxim Magazine*, December 2008.

18 Will Leitch, 'Shades of Brando: Mickey Rourke's Odd Career, Reborn with "*The Wrestler*," Is Curiously Familiar', *New York Magazine*, 29 September 2008.

19 Sheila O'Malley, 'Mickey Rourke: The Vagaries of Genius', *The Sheila Variations*, 26 September 2008. Available at: http://www.sheilaomalley.com/?p=8445. (Italics in original.)

20 Peter Travers, 'Iron Man 2', *Rolling Stone*, 30 April 2010.

21 Roger Ebert, 'Iron Man 2', *Chicago Sun-Times*, 5 May 2010.

22 Marc Grief, 'What Was the Hipster?', *New York Magazine*, 24 October 2010.

23 Darren Aronofsky, quoted in Sheila Johnston, 'Mickey Rourke Bounces Back off the Ropes', *Telegraph*, 2 January 2009.

24 LaSalle, '*Sin City*'.

25 Cintra Wilson, 'Mickey Rourke's Desperate Truths', *Salon*, 15 May 2002. Available at: http://www.salon.com/2002/15/rourke.

26 Pauline Kael, 'Marlon Brando: An American Hero', in *Kiss Kiss Bang Bang* (New York and Boston: Little, Brown and Company, 1968), p. 192.

BIBLIOGRAPHY

'9½ Weeks', *Montreal Gazette*, 15 March 1986.

Abramovitch, Seth, 'Parents Outraged as Annie Leibovitz Sexualizes Mickey Rourke for Her Art', *Defamer*, 4 February 2009. Available at: http://gawker.com/5146339/parents-outraged-as-annie-leibovitz-sexualizes-mickey-rourke-for-her-art.

Andrews, David, *Soft in the Middle: The Contemporary Softcore Feature in Its Contexts* (Columbus: Ohio State University Press, 2006).

Barthes, Roland, 'The World of Wrestling', in *Mythologies*, trans. Annette Lavers (New York: Farrar, Straus and Giroux, 1972), pp. 15–25.

Bennett, Ray, 'Passion Play', *Hollywood Reporter*, 14 October 2010.

Benson, Sheila, '"Dragon": A Compelling Look Inside Chinatown', *LA Times*, 16 August 1985.

Benson, Sheila, '9½ Weeks', *LA Times*, 21 February 1986.

Biacolli, Amy, '*The Wrestler*', *Houston Chronicle*, 15 January 2009.

Boyar, Jay, '9½ Weeks', *Orlando Sentinel*, 19 April 1986.

Bradshaw, Peter, '*The Wrestler*', *Guardian*, 15 January 2009.

Brando, Marlon, with Robert Lindsay, *Songs My Mother Taught Me* (Toronto: Random House, 1994).

Bukowksi, Charles, *Hollywood* (New York: Ecco, 2002; first published 1989).

B.W., 'Sin City', *Time Out London*, no. 1815, 1–8 June 2005.

Canby, Vincent, '"9½ Weeks," a Sexual Journey', *New York Times*, 21 February 1986.

Canby, Vincent, 'Angel Heart', *New York Times*, 6 March 1987.

Crocker, Jonathan, '*The Wrestler*: Rourke Gets Real in Aronofsky's Stripped-Down Bodyslammer', *Total Film: The Guide to Modern Movies*, 28 April 2009.

Dargis, Manohla, 'Sin City', *New York Times*, 1 April 2005.

Drake, Tim, 'Actor Mickey Rourke Says a Priest Saved His Life', *National Catholic Register*, 8 October 2009.

Dyer, Richard, 'Coming Out as Going In: The Image of the Homosexual as a Sad Young Man', in *The Culture of Queers* (London: Routledge, 2002), pp. 116–36.

Dylan, Bob, *Chronicles: Volume One* (New York: Simon and Schuster, 2005).

Ebert, Roger, 'Angel Heart', *Chicago Sun-Times*, 6 March 1987.

Ebert, Roger, '*The Wrestler*', *Chicago Sun-Times*, 23 December 2008.

French, Philip, 'Sin City', *Observer*, 4 June 2005.

Garbarino, Steve, 'The Resurrection of Mickey Rourke', *Maxim Magazine*, December 2008.

Golding, Sue, 'James Dean: The Almost Perfect Lesbian Hermaphrodite', in Tessa Boffin and Jean Fraser (eds), *Stolen Glances: Lesbians Take Photographs* (London: Pandora, 1991), pp. 197–202.

Hansen, Miriam, 'Pleasure, Ambivalence, Identification: Valentino and Female Spectatorship', in Leo Braudy and Marshall Cohen (eds), *Film Theory and Criticism* (New York: OUP, 2004; first published 1974), pp. 643–51.

Harris, Christopher, '9½ Weeks', *Ottawa Citizen*, 5 April 1988.

Heard, Christopher, *Mickey Rourke: High and Low* (Medford, NJ: Plexus Publishing, 2006).

Heilman, Jeremy, 'Passion Play', *Moviemartyr.com*, 14 July 2011. Available at: http://www.moviemartyr.com/2010/passionplay.htm.

Hinton, S. E., *Rumble Fish* (New York: Laurel Leaf, 1989).

Huddleston, Tom, '*The Wrestler*', *Time Out London*, 15–24 January 2009.

Japhy, Grant, 'Mickey Rourke Super Sorry He's a Homophobic Asshole', *Queerty*, 11 November 2008. Available at: http://www.queerty.com/mickey-rourke-sorry-hes-a-homophobic-asshole-20081111/.

Johnston, Sheila, 'Mickey Rourke Bounces Back off the Ropes', *Telegraph*, 2 January 2009.

Jordan, Pat, 'His Fists Are Up, and His Guard Is Down', *New York Times*, 28 November 2008.

Kael, Pauline, 'Marlon Brando: An American Hero', in *Kiss Kiss Bang Bang* (New York and Boston: Little, Brown and Company, 1968), pp. 189–95.

Kael, Pauline, '*Body Heat*', in *5001 Nights at the Movies* (New York: Henry Holt and Company, 1991).

Kael, Pauline, '*Diner*', in *For Keeps* (New York: Plume, 1996).

Kempley, Rita, '*Angel Heart*', *Washington Post*, 6 March 1987.

Kohn, Eric, 'Megan Fox, Mickey Rourke and Bill Murray Lose Direction in Awful "Passion Play"', *Indiewire*, 3 May 2011. Available at: http://www. indiewire.com/article/review_megan_fox_mickey_rourke_and_bill_ murray_lose_direction_in_awful_pass.

Lane, Anthony, '*The Wrestler*', *New Yorker*, 22 December 2008.

LaSalle, Mick, '*Sin City*', *San Francisco Chronicle*, 1 April 2005.

Leitch, Will, 'Shades of Brando: Mickey Rourke's Odd Career, Reborn with "*The Wrestler*," Is Curiously Familiar', *New York Magazine*, 29 September 2008.

Lott, Eric, *Love and Theft: Blackface Minstrelsy and the White Working Class* (Oxford: Oxford University Press, 1995).

McNeill, Elizabeth, *Nine and a Half Weeks: A Memoir of a Love Affair* (New York, E. P. Dutton, 1978; reprint 2005).

Mahler, Richard, 'On the Set: On "The Last Outlaw's" Trail: HBO Shoots 'Em up in New Mexico', *LA Times*, 24 October 1993.

Mailer, Norman, *The White Negro* (San Francisco: City Lights Books, 1957).

Maslin, Janet, '*Rumble Fish* (1983)', *New York Times*, 7 October 1983.

Matthews, Tom, '9½ *Weeks*', *Boxoffice*, 1 April 1986.

Millar, Jeff, '9½ *Weeks*', *Houston Chronicle*, 18 April 1986.

Miller, Leslie Adrienne, 'After an Evening with Mickey Rourke I Pick up Petrarch', *Mississippi Review* vol. 27 no. 1–2, 1998, pp. 14–16.

Morris, Mark, '9½ Weeks', *Observer*, 4 May 1990.

Morris, Sophie, 'Mickey Rourke: The Bruiser Is Back', *Independent*, 3 January 2009.

Mueller, Elaine, 'Love in the Hamptons', *New Yorker*, 29 July 1972.

Mulvey, Laura, 'Visual Pleasure and Narrative Cinema', reprinted in *Visual and Other Pleasures* (Basingstoke, Hants.: Palgrave, 2009), pp. 14–30.

O'Malley, Sheila, 'Mickey Rourke: The Vagaries of Genius', *The Sheila Variations*, 26 September 2008. Available at: http://www.sheilaomalley.com/?p=8445.

O'Malley, Sheila, 'Gone Away, Come Back: Mickey Rourke', *Slant*, 17 December 2008. Available at: http://www.slantmagazine.com/house/2008/17/gone-away-come-back-mickey-rourke.

O'Malley, Sheila, 'Through the Fishtank: Mickey Rourke in *The Rainmaker*', *The Sheila Variations*, 27 December 2008. Available at: http://www.sheilaomalley.com/?p=8730.

Otis, Carré and Hugo Schwyzer, *Beauty, Disrupted: A Memoir* (New York: HarperCollins It Books, 2011).

Price, S. L., 'Much Ado about Nothing: How Barry Levinson's *Diner* Changed Cinema, 30 Years Later', *Vanity Fair*, March 2012.

Raab, Scott, 'Mickey Rourke', *Real Hollywood Stories* (New York: Tatra Press/BoCo Media, 2008).

Rempala, Dan, *Everything I Need to Know, I Learned from Mickey Rourke Movies* (Bloomington, IN: Xlibris Corp, 2009).

Rodriguez, Rene, *The Wrestler*, *Miami Herald*, n.d.

Rosenbaum, Jonathan, 'Barfly', *Chicago Reader*, n.d.

Rothkopf, Joshua, 'Passion Play', *Time Out*, 3 May 2011.

Russell, Candice, 'Steamy Saga Nothing but a Tease', *Fort Lauderdale Sun Sentinel*, 21 April 1986.

Savran, David, *Taking It Like a Man: White Masculinity, Masochism, and Contemporary American Culture* (Princeton, NJ: Princeton University Press, 2008).

Scott, Jay, '9½ Weeks', *Globe and Mail*, 21 February 1986.

Shail, Andrew and Robin Stoate, *Back to the Future* (London: BFI, 2010).

Smatysia, 'Barfly', *Moviesonline.com*, n.d. Available at: http://www.3movies online.com/Barfly-1987-movie.

Sontag, Susan, 'Notes on Camp', in *Against Interpretation* (New York: Picador, 1966), pp. 275–92.

Stanislavski, Konstantin, *An Actor's Work: A Student's Diary*, trans. Jean
    Benedetti (New York: Routledge, 2009).

Stanley, Alessandra, 'Can 50 Million Frenchmen Be Wrong?', *New York
    Times*, 21 October 1990.

Tait, Robert, 'Hollywood Film Accused of Insulting Iran', *Guardian*,
    12 December 2008.

Travers, Peter, '*Sin City*', *Rolling Stone*, 1 April 2005.

Travers, Peter, 'Iron Man 2', *Rolling Stone*, 30 April 2010.

Tucker, Ken, 'Sin City', *New York Magazine*, 21 May 2005.

Turan, Kenneth, 'As Fake as Wrestling', *LA Times*, 17 December 2008.

Vineberg, Steve, *Method Actors: Three Generations of an American Acting Style*
    (New York: Schirmer Trade Books, 1994).

Walden, Robert, 'The Method and the Myth', *Backstage*, 21 April 2009.

Warner, Kara, 'Megan Fox Clarifies Mickey Rourke Tattoo', *MTVnews*,
    17 September 2010.

Weiss, Margot D., 'Mainstreaming Kink: The Politics of Popular BDSM
    Representation in U.S. Popular Media', *Journal of Homosexuality* vol. 50
    no. 2–3, pp. 103–30.

Williams, Kent, 'The Wrestler: Mickey Rourke Toughens Up', *Isthmus*,
    16 January 2009.

Williams, Linda, 'Studying Soft Sex', *Film Quarterly* vol. 62 no. 1, 2008,
    pp. 86–8.

Williams, Linda Ruth, *The Erotic Thriller in Contemporary Cinema*
    (Bloomington: Indiana University Press, 2005).

Wilson, Cintra, 'Mickey Rourke's Desperate Truths', *Salon*, 15 May 2002.
    Available at: http://www.salon.com/2002/15/rourke.

Zacharek, Stephanie, 'Here's Looking at You, Comeback Kids', *Salon*,
    20 February 2009. Available at: http://www.salon.com/2009/02/20/
    rourke_downey/.

FILMOGRAPHY

LOVE IN THE HAMPTONS (short) (Tom Folino, USA, 1976), Swede.

1941 (Steven Spielberg, USA, 1979), Reese.

FADE TO BLACK (Vernon Zimmerman, USA, 1980), Richie.

HEAVEN'S GATE (Michael Cimino, USA, 1980), Nick Ray.

BODY HEAT (Lawrence Kasdan, USA, 1981), Teddy Lewis.

DINER (Barry Levinson, USA, 1982), Robert 'Boogie' Sheftell.

EUREKA (Nicolas Roeg, UK/USA, 1983), Aurelio D'Amato.

RUMBLE FISH (Francis Ford Coppola, USA, 1983), The Motorcycle Boy.

THE POPE OF GREENWICH VILLAGE (Stuart Rosenberg, USA, 1984),
    Charlie Moran.

YEAR OF THE DRAGON (Michael Cimino, USA, 1985), Stanley White.

9½ WEEKS (Adrian Lyne, USA, 1986), John.

ANGEL HEART (Alan Parker, USA/Canada/UK, 1987), Harry Angel.

BARFLY (Barbet Schroeder, USA, 1987), Henry Chinaski.

A PRAYER FOR THE DYING (Mike Hodges, UK, 1987), Martin Fallon.

HOMEBOY (Michael Seresin, USA, 1988), Johnny Walker.

FRANCESCO (Liliana Cavani, Italy/West Germany, 1989), Francesco.

JOHNNY HANDSOME (Walter Hill, USA, 1989), John 'Johnny
    Handsome' Sedly/Johnny Mitchell.

DESPERATE HOURS (Michael Cimino, USA, 1990), Michael Bosworth.

WILD ORCHID (Zalman King, USA, 1990), James Wheeler.

HARLEY DAVIDSON AND THE MARLBORO MAN (Simon Wincer,
    USA, 1991), Harley Davidson.

WHITE SANDS (Roger Donaldson, USA, 1992), Goran Lennox.

F.T.W. (Michael Karbelnikoff, USA, 1994), Frank T. Wells.

FALL TIME (Paul Warner, USA, 1995), Florence.

BULLET (Julien Temple, USA, 1996), Butch 'Bullet' Stein.

EXIT IN RED (Yurek Bogayevicz, USA, 1996), Ed Altman.

ANOTHER 9½ WEEKS (Anne Goursand, France/UK/USA, 1997), John Gray.

DOUBLE TEAM (Hark Tsui, USA, 1997), Stavros.

THE RAINMAKER (Francis Ford Coppola, USA, 1997), Bruiser Stone.

BUFFALO '66 (Vincent Gallo, USA, 1998), The Bookie.

POINT BLANK (Matt Earl Beasley, USA, 1998), Rudy Ray.

THURSDAY (Skip Woods, USA, 1998), Kasarov.

OUT IN FIFTY (Bojesse Christopher and Scott Anthony Leet, USA, 1999), Jack Bracken.

SHADES (Erik Van Looy, Belgium, 1999), Paul S. Sullivan.

SHERGAR (Dennis C. Lewiston, UK/USA, 1999), Gavin O'Rourke.

ANIMAL FACTORY (Steve Buscemi, USA, 2000), Jan the Actress.

GET CARTER (Stephen Kay, USA, 2000), Cyrus Paice.

THE FOLLOW (short) (Wong Kar-wai, USA, 2001), Husband.

PICTURE CLAIRE (Bruce McDonald, Canada/USA, 2001), Eddie.

THE PLEDGE (Sean Penn, USA, 2001), Jim Olstad.

THEY CRAWL (John Allardice, USA, 2001), Tiny Frakes.

SPUN (Jonas Åkerlund, USA, 2002), The Cook.

MASKED AND ANONYMOUS (Larry Charles, USA/UK, 2003), Edmund.

ONCE UPON A TIME IN MEXICO (Robert Rodriguez, USA, 2003), Billy.

MAN ON FIRE (Tony Scott, USA/UK, 2004), Jordan.

DOMINO (Tony Scott, France/USA/UK, 2005), Ed Moseby.

SIN CITY (Frank Miller, Robert Rodriguez and Quentin Tarantino, USA, 2005), Marv.

ALEX RIDER: OPERATION STORMBREAKER (Geoffrey Sax, Germany/USA/UK, 2006), Darrius Sayle.

THE INFORMERS (Gregor Jordan, USA, 2008), Peter.

KILLSHOT (John Madden, USA, 2008), Armand 'Blackbird' Degas.

THE WRESTLER (Darren Aronofsky, USA/France, 2008), Randy 'The Ram' Robinson.

13 (Géla Babluani, USA, 2010), Jefferson.

THE EXPENDABLES (Sylvester Stallone, USA, 2010), Tool.

IRON MAN 2 (Jon Favreau, USA, 2010), Ivan Vanko.

PASSION PLAY (Mitch Glazer, USA, 2010), Nate Poole.

BLACK GOLD (Jeta Amata, Nigeria, 2011), Craig Hudson.

IMMORTALS (Tarsem Singh, USA, 2011), King Hyperion.

THE COURIER (Hany Abu-Assad, USA, 2012), Maxwell.

BLACK NOVEMBER (Jeta Amata, Nigeria, 2012), Tom Hudson.

JAVA HEAT (Conor Allyn, USA, 2013), Malik.

DEAD IN TOMBSTONE (Roel Reiné, USA, 2013), Blacksmith.

SIN CITY: A DAME TO KILL FOR (Frank Miller, Robert Rodriguez, USA, 2014), Marv.

SKIN TRAFFIK (Ara Paiaya, UK, 2014), Vogel.

INDEX

Note: Page numbers in **bold** indicate detailed analysis. Those in *italic* refer to illustrations. *n* = endnote.

List of Illustrations

While considerable effort has been made to correctly identify the copyright holders, this has not been possible in all cases. We apologise for any apparent negligence, and any omissions or corrections brought to our attention will be remedied in any future editions.